THINK AMERICA. THINK!

I dedicate this book to my parents. To my late father, Ferenc Ledniczky, who heroically lost his life at the end of World War II while removing "booby trapped" improvised explosive devices (IED) so families can safely to return to their homes. To my mother, Julianna Ledniczky, who has always believed that someday I would create something that would be worthwhile and worthy of the world's notice.

THINK AMERICA. THINK!
Put Your Brain In Gear Before Engaging Your Mouth

A Political Treatise
by:
Ferenc A. Ledniczky

Published by:

BOOKSURGE LLC
An Amazon.com company

ISBN: 1 – 4196 – 2369 - 9

Published by
BookSurge Publishing
A division of BookSurge, LLC. an Amazon.com company
5341 Dorchester Road, Suite 16
Charleston, South Carolina 29418
1-866-308-6235

To order additional copies, please contact us.
BookSurge, LLC.
1 800 308-6235
orders@booksurge.com

I want to thank my family for their tolerance and patience while I was so preoccupied with the writing of this book.

Thanks to my editor and ghostwriter, LaRue Foster, who helped me take the "Hungarian" out of my sentences and to translate my thoughts into real English. A special thanks to Joel Barbee for putting his magic pen to "paper" to produce the art work that helped me to visually express something I could only imagine and describe in words.

CONTENTS

WAR WITH BULLETS

Right vs. Wrong

WAR TO PREVENT WAR

Nuclear War Must Be Avoided

Preempting the Enemy

Are We Safe Yet

Weapon of Peace

Cold War Two is in Progress

"Today, with only the United States in a position of real power, the industrialized nations of the world are concerned with our ultimate intentions..."

Friends vs. Friends

"In today's global political climate, the primary reason behind most modern wars – both "cold" and "hot" – is economic survival..."

Power Shift

"When the Soviet Union collapsed, that left just one super power with the technology, wealth, and internal dynamics capable of ..."

The Power of One

"There is nothing we can do about the attitude of other nations at the present time but continue on our present path. Why? The hatred of other nations, many of them our professed allies in times past, is based on fear of American power they cannot influence..."

Historical Roots

"European nations are basing their current attitudes on negative experience with their own strong governments in the past, none of which were truly democratic in nature. In Europe, countries both large and small were for many centuries under control of absolute monarchies and dictatorships..."

CHAPTER TWO
"L'Enfant Terrible?"

Leader Dependent Societies

Our Leader - Neutral Democracy

America's Success

American Cradle

Constitutional Protection

CHAPTER THREE
Wherever We Are, There We Are

One Vote

"Democratic governments represent the views and values of society as a whole, or more specifically, the views and values of that segment of society that makes its wishes known... "

The Price of Freedom

"The freedom we enjoy today was dearly bought by the sacrifices of our founding fathers when, in the words of the Declaration of Independence, they pledged their "lives, their fortunes, and their sacred honor" so that we would have the right to choose our leaders..."

We Reap What We Sow

"If we sow nothing, we may have a sorry harvest indeed, based on the decisions made by others which affect our personal well-being..."

Our Politicians

"Politicians are wonderfully facile individuals, who are born chameleons by nature, ready to tell us what we want to hear but not necessarily what we need to know..."

What if...?

"What if, just once, the politician who is soliciting our votes tells us not what we want to hear but rather..."

What We Need to Know

"Each elected politician is the product of our choice. And by our willingness only to hear magical solutions to our country's problems, we are deluding ourselves by..."

CHAPTER FOUR
Our Influence

The Nucleus

Thinking in a Bubble

The Globalization of American Interest

When America Sneezes

The Globalization of Commerce

America's Global Politics

Is There a Runner Up

CHAPTER FIVE
The Journey

Where We Go From Here

The Test of Time

Our Potential Weakness

The Price We Pay

Our Security Blanket

We Are the "Boatman"

Participate or Just Enjoy the "Ride"

Be Eternally Vigilant

CHAPTER SIX
Information or Conformation

Think America. Think!

Think For Yourself

Our Values in Communication

Information Galore

Our Hidden Agenda

The Voice of Authority

Put Your Brain in Gear

APPENDIX

Foreword

Dr. Albert Schweitzer, the noted Nobel Prize winner, Philosopher, Theologian, and Humanitarian, was asked by someone, "What's wrong with people today?" He answered, "People simply don't think."

—

We Americans have so much to be proud of and happy about; we have created the richest land on Earth with freedom and lifestyles that are the envy of other nations. We are always eager to share our wealth with others and anxious to right all wrongs wherever we can.

In spite of our accomplishments, our country is still a baby in the length of its history, and most of the countries of the world see us as a very strong, but stumbling, giant toddler. The youth of our country is also reflected in our behavior. Many of us have a tendency to speak our minds without thinking, thereby sometimes confusing others and angering ourselves unnecessarily.

The objective of this book is to convince you, the reader, to think before accepting statements made by others as true. Apart from watching the evening news, many of us are uninformed about what is going on in our country and in the world beyond our shores. We need to know that our nation, for all its super power status, is part of a larger world, where the attitudes and actions of other nations affect everything here at home, from the price of sneakers to the cost of our military spending.

Not understanding the political scene around us can come to be very costly for America. In the following pages of this book you will be challenged to consider the issues of national and global politics, to become engaged in the decisions that affect you and the future of our country.

You should make it a habit to view things in their proper context and take time to see each issue from different perspectives. You will save yourself from anxiety, unhappiness or unwarranted joy and happiness, followed by disappointment.

You will feel a lot better about yourself and the rest of the world if you just take time to think for a moment instead being swayed by each perpetually changing *crisis du-jour*.

However, keep in mind that there is no logical answer to an emotional issue. In other words, if one believes in something, no fact or logical explanation will be likely to sway that belief. One must be willing to be open minded, engage in a logical debate, and be willing to accept and welcome the outcome as an answer to the issue at hand.

Try to separate what you believe in from what is logical. Although people talk about facts, opinions, or personal observations, you still should use your own judgment.

In this book I address past, present, and future issues about our country, our history, politics, war, battles, and our place in world society.

CHAPTER ONE
Victory

Wars and Battles

Throughout history, with all of its horrors and destruction, people were fighting battles in wars to right wrongs or conquer other lands and people.

The 4th day of July in 1776 was the day when this "baby" nation declared its independence and called itself The United States of America. In 1783, this new nation was born out of the ashes and fallen heroes of a horrible war and at last began to consolidate its victory against England.

Unforeseen at that time was that in a little more than 200 years, this "Baby" would become the most dominant and powerful nation on earth. Unlike any other country in the world, this country's power rises from the creativity and freedom of its citizens and is supported by the rule of law as defined in the Constitution.

This country is ready and willing to use its power, not to colonize or conquer other nations, but to teach them the value of freedom and democracy. In its quest to show the world the value of freedom, this young country has already and will be forced in the future to fight the enemies of freedom.

Considering our history, our economic and military power, and determination of the citizens of this country, it appears that the United States has already won all past and future wars.

Think about this statement for a moment. It is historically proven that the outcome is fixed, even before a war begins. For the U.S. the only variable is the "price" that we as a country have already paid in the past and will pay in the future to win our battles.

The inherent rule is that the country with the strongest sustainable economy always wins the war. Consequently, only a country with a decidedly stronger economy would be able to entertain the thought of confronting the United States with the hope of winning.

No other country in the world has an economy that can hope to ever match that of the United States.

Wars

War is a political confrontation between countries for ideological and/or economic reasons. It may or may not involve an armed conflict with bullets, which is called a battle.

For the sake of this discussion, it is important to understand the distinction between war and battle. We often use the two terms interchangeably, but there is a difference between being at war and being in a battle. We can be in a battle without being at war -- and we can be in a war without having a single armed conflict. In past centuries, war always meant actual battles. Today the leaders of the warring parties may smile at each other, covering up their intent, and a physical confrontation may never take place.

Today a war via economic and social pressure without bullets is called a "Cold War."

Battles

A battle is a physical confrontation between countries and adversaries and may or may not be part of a war. A battle may involve both soldiers and civilians. There may not be a clear beginning or end to a battle. The outcome may be a clear victory for one side, but sometimes the fighting just ends without a victor.

In Vietnam, war was never declared by the United States or by Vietnam. Instead, a series of armed conflicts took place over ten years. Before the U.S. entered that conflict, the French had fought in Vietnam also, and finally gave up their battle for that country. There was no clear outcome.

Like the U.S., the French simply stopped fighting and went home after a long conflict where there was no decisive victory for either side. In 1974, the U.S. evacuated its troops, leaving the country to the North Vietnamese Communist regime.

The long and terribly costly struggle for the U.S. in Vietnam was simply a military conflict without any declaration of war. When the shooting stops, the battle is over.

War with Bullets

In World War II, "D-Day" was a clearly victorious battle as part of a war. The United States was at war with both Germany and Japan, a time marked by bloody conflicts for four long years. We decisively won that war. Following World War II, the United States consolidated its winnings.

The losing countries had to submit to the rules of political conduct dictated by the winner. In 1945, Germany and Japan signed documents of surrender with America, which dictated the terms of surrender for those countries, including rules by which those nations would conduct themselves in government, business in general, and international relations -- and the United States had the power to enforce their compliance.

In short, the United States consolidated its winnings by changing the way Germany and Japan would be governed until those nations stabilized and were not in a position to successfully wage war again against the United States.

Instruments of War

There are three major instruments of war: armies, money, and law. Armies may be used as an active force against an adversary or as a threat in reserve. Money provides a foundation that enables one country to sustain operations longer than its adversary can.

The law of the land serves as a cohesive force, keeping the country united so that people mutually understand and respect the role each citizen will play.

Armies

The reality is that armies can't win or lose wars; they can only kill people and destroy things through battles. They are *instruments* of war. The objective of any army is to deny the enemy the resources, manpower, and the will to resist, ultimately causing the country to capitulate.

In the Cold War that followed World War II, the military arm of the U.S. was a static instrument -- chiefly as a threat held in reserve against other nations. Our armed forces never actively engaged the U.S.S.R. or its successor nations in battle.

Today, knowing the power of the American military strength is a powerful deterrent to other nations who might consider engaging in armed conflict against the U.S.

Money

In the 1600s, the Italian-born general, Raimondo Montecuccoli, said of his experience in the Thirty Years War, that it takes three things to win a war: **Money, Money** — and more **Money!**

Money makes the difference and establishes the winner even before the war starts or before the first call to battle is sounded. The winner is fixed. The game is rigged to favor the side that can afford to pay the cost of the war.

The country that can best afford to fight battles or fight a war of economic attrition will eventually win. Consequently, the country with the best sustainable economy will always win a war by fighting a war of attrition -- draining the other side of its resources over time, with or without battles. In such a war, the nation may even lose many or most of the battles, as America did in the American Revolution against the British. Yet America still won that war.

In the American Revolution, both time and distance worked in favor of our new nation. The British had to import troops and supplies, at first believing that with the appearance of armed soldiers, many of the colonists would join them in securing order again under British rule. But a number of factors worked against an ultimate British victory.

The Americans did not go over to the British side as expected, a major error in Britain's political view of America as an unruly colony where the people would welcome established British order.

Supply lines were thin, and it took months to cross the Atlantic, depending on prevailing winds and weather. Britain even had difficulty in recruiting sufficient number of soldiers because many British soldiers thought of Americans as British citizens and did not relish the idea of fighting their own countrymen. This meant hiring Hessian mercenaries to fight the war alongside the British troops.

At that time, Britain was the strongest military power in the world, but still they lost the war. Americans had a powerful incentive to win, even though their untrained militia could not always match Britain's troops in numbers or equipment. They knew if they lost, their hard-won property and even their lives would be forfeited.

Americans won few of the actual armed conflicts, but distance, time, supplies and even less motivated troops caused Britain to yield to America. And it was a decisive victory for the new nation. America consolidated its winnings and formed a strong Constitutional government. We decisively won the war.

In the American Revolution, the concept of declaring our independence, as well as choosing the time and place to form a new country, guaranteed success. Once we declared independence, France was put in the position by default of helping us.

France could not allow the British to win and expand their empire. After that war, *the U.S. consolidated its winnings* by enacting the U.S. Constitution, and soon thereafter, the Bill of Rights.

Britain tried once more in the War of 1812 and learned the same lesson again: time, distance, and thin supply lines made it impossible to conquer the United States of America.

America consolidated its winnings again and gained a decisive victory, then forged a treaty with Britain which benefited both countries and resulted thereafter in a strong alliance between the two nations. Britain finally recognized America as a strong world power that it could not defeat.

Soldiers Win Battles
Money Wins Wars

We have only to look at the internal conflict fought by Americans in the Civil War to show clearly the difference that superior resources make in a war, which requires huge amounts of money.

When war was declared by the United States government against the Confederate States who had declared their independence, the outcome of the war was already decided.

In the early 1800s, the North began to expand its cities with manufacturing and the creation of finished goods for sale. Instead of growing their own food in farming communities, the North began to rely on the purchase of raw materials, foodstuffs, and other supplies, and developed an economy based on manufacturing.

They built over 100 miles of railroad to transport those goods to over one mile in the South. Their wealth arose from the goods and services the people bought and sold and traded internationally through their deep-water Atlantic coastal ports.

The South developed differently, with the focus on establishing large plantations where tobacco and cotton were major crops beyond foodstuffs. Both tobacco and cotton were sold raw and exported. The land was the major wealth in the South and that wealth was in the hands of a single upper class that had little interest in building factories or markets for goods that were shipped abroad or to the Northern states for processing.

Although some labor-saving inventions were already available, such as Eli Whitney's cotton gin, there was little incentive in the South to establish an urban economy fueled by factories, machinery, and workers for hire. The South also lacked a skilled labor supply. Most people, even the wealthiest, were engaged in farming, whether on large plantations or on small farms.

Even if the South at the start of the Civil War had begun to establish manufacturing centers for making weapons, increasing the miles of rails for shipment of goods and transport of military troops, it was already too late.

The South was too far behind to catch up. Equipping Confederate troops and arming them required an outlay of capital abroad to secure essential supplies, and many nations were reluctant to make alliances with this new political entity, fearing future reprisals from the United States when the conflict was over.

The Confederate money coined by the South was not backed by gold as were United States dollars, so the currency would purchase little in world trade markets.

This lack of foresight cost the South dearly over four long years of warfare. The few manufacturers that did exist in the South were largely a class of artisans who made essential goods for plantation use, printers who produced newspapers and other publications, and craftsmen who made furniture, and farm implements, largely by hand labor.

Yet if generals, not money, won wars, the outcome of the Civil War might have been quite different. Some of West Point's finest graduates were generals in the Confederacy, returning to their native states to protect homes and families that were dear to them. Robert E. Lee, Pierre G. T. Beauregard, and "Stonewall" Jackson were among the best military strategists who ever attended West Point.

President Lincoln was plagued by a series of inept, indecisive leaders; beginning with General McClellan, until halfway through the war, when Generals William Tecumseh Sherman and Ulysses S. Grant were placed in charge of the North's military campaigns. The tide of battles then began to turn in the North's favor and never wavered thereafter.

Without a change of generals, however, would the North have won? Absolutely! The South was quickly drained of resources and food supplies. Due to Northern blockades of Southern ports, there was no way to re-supply men in the field with foreign arms, clothing, and medicines for wounds.

Even its large plantation economy for food and raw trading goods fell apart because the war was largely fought on Southern soil. Every able-bodied man was called on to join the Confederate Army, with no organized labor force to harvest crops, much less prepare them for transport to army depots for distribution. Many of the plantations were ravaged by both Union and Confederate armies on the move who took any and all available food supplies with them as they swept through the land.

The Northern side had won the war even before the first shot was fired on U.S. Army troops at Fort Sumter in 1861. The North could afford to pay the immediate cost and to continue to pay it over a long time if necessary in order to win. The South lacked the capital and the ability to raise it to sustain a lengthy war of attrition.

Later on, during World War II, the United States faced its greatest test in a global war against Germany, Japan, and their allies. At the start of the conflict, America was ill-prepared in terms of up-to-date weaponry, ships, and ground equipment. When the war first started in Europe, America had hoped to stay out of the war, still remembering the issues confronted in World War I. But when Japan launched its attack on Pearl Harbor, it became clear that we could no longer hope to remain isolated.

Once again, America proved itself to be able to mobilize rapidly and to create new superior technology to fight back.

In just a few short months, the entire economy was converted into a wartime defense producer. Factories retooled to build airplanes, new ships, and produce arms. And in the sleepy little town of Oak Ridge, Tennessee, and at Los Alamos, New Mexico, a massive program was launched to develop a new, more powerful weapon than the world had ever known before -- the atomic bomb. America's young men enlisted in the armed forces by the thousands, not waiting to be drafted. Women went to work in defense factories, ably performing work that no woman had ever done before. Families accepted gas rationing, planted victory gardens, and bought "Victory Bonds" to support the country's need for money to build strong defenses.

The first few months of the war were a military disaster for Americans, fighting with outmoded equipment until the factories began producing new armaments. But by 1942, the tide of battle began to turn in America's favor as planes and tanks and guns rolled off retooled assembly lines and we scored our first major victory in the Pacific at the Battle of Midway.

We were also able to support our European allies, chiefly Great Britain, launching an invading force against the Axis powers and begin bombing raids over German-held strongholds throughout Europe. In less than a year after Pearl Harbor, America was fully militarized and was supplying our allies with equipment as well as our own forces.

No other nation on the face of the earth could have mobilized so quickly. America alone possessed the internal resources to arm and deploys forces across the globe.

While victory was still three years away, by 1942 the U.S. fielded armaments and men on a scale never before imagined. That ability meant that winning the war was a foregone conclusion, even before the atomic bomb became a reality in 1945. We had the best military tacticians in both theaters of war:

General Douglas McArthur in the Pacific, Generals Omar Bradley, Dwight Eisenhower and George Patton in Europe were commanding forces for the successful D-Day invasion at Normandy. With the detonation of the atomic bomb in Nagasaki and Hiroshima in 1945, victory over Japan was almost immediate. Our power and reach proved to be superior to that available anywhere else in the world.

But even without the atomic bomb and our outstanding military leadership, would the U.S. have still won WW II? Absolutely! The war would have probably taken longer and would have cost significantly more in human lives, but we would have won in any case.

By 1942, the U.S. was the only country with a fully functioning industrial base and shores secure from invasion. We remained out of range of our enemies, and never again in the war did a foreign power manage a direct attack against America as Japan did in 1941.

After the war, America alone had the resources to help the war-torn nations in Europe rebuild their economies by enacting the Marshall Plan. Single-handedly, America launched the Berlin airlift to provide relief and vital food and medical supplies to keep our former enemies from starvation.

We produced enough food to feed those in need, who would have perished in the dark days after the war when their economies were in shambles. Superior technology and abundant natural resources made America victorious in World War II -- and those same resources keep America the most powerful and the richest nation in the world today.

Law of the Land

U nlike other societies where nations are dependent on the power and influence of one person,
our ultimate weapon is our law of the land. It for-
mally establishes the way our nation and people gov-
ern themselves and the way they respond to internal
or external threats to our country's well being.

The Constitution of the
United States of America

A lthough the United States has demonstrated its
superior economic power, the underlying basis
for American success does not lie only in money and
military strength. It lies instead in the inspired vision
of a powerful document, which has often been copied
in part by other nations but never equaled. That
document is the Constitution of the United States.
The men who drafted that document were inspired as
they shepherded it through the process of becoming
the fundamental law and basis for American government over the past two centuries.

They were men of vision, but they were also
practical men, who understood human nature and
had the common sense to establish a workable document that provided checks and balances on governmental power so that the young nation in their care
would be unlikely to fall under the influence of a
demagogue or a tyrant. They knew the wisdom of

Voltaire who said:*"Power corrupts, and absolute power corrupts absolutely."* Their goal was to create a body of law that would prevent any one person or branch of government from being able to overthrow the other branches.

Limited Power
Protected Rights

Our Founding Fathers understood that all power in the hands of men must be limited. Most of them had memories of living under a monarchy and wanted to prevent that type of absolute rule from ever happening in America.

We will explore the Constitution and the role it plays in ensuring the continued existence of the United States government in more detail in later chapters; for now, let's take a look at some of the fundamentals it provides.

Each branch of government -- the legislative, the executive, and the judiciary -- has limited powers, and each one has the ability to check actions by the others.

- Only the U.S. Congress can enact laws.
- The President can veto any law Congress enacts.
- Congress can override the President's veto by a two-thirds majority vote.
- The President's power is to enforce the laws made by Congress.

- The Supreme Court reviews and determines the Constitutionality of any law enacted when it is challenged.

The Bill of Rights

But even with the passage of the Constitution, there were key personal rights of the people that required protection, and the first ten amendments to the Constitution -- the Bill of Rights -- completed the task our Founding Fathers began.

During the debates on the adoption of the Constitution, opponents of the Constitution repeatedly charged that the document as drafted would create a central government whose powers, if misused, could result in tyranny.

They remembered all too well the way in which the British had quartered troops in their homes, stopped due process of law, and otherwise threatened the homes and safety of Americans.

To stop this possibility in the future, they demanded a "Bill of Rights" that would spell out the rights and protections for American citizens. In response to these concerns, the first Congress of the United States enacted the first ten amendments to the Constitution which we know today as the Bill of Rights.

These rights included freedom of worship with no state religion, freedom of speech by citizens and by the press, and freedom of assembly, the right to bear arms for protection and prohibitions against quartering military in civilian homes. Citizens also have judicially protected rights, such as protection from unlawful search and seizure of themselves or their possessions, and if accused of a crime, the right to a speedy trial, without excessive bail. Crimes within a state and not against the federal government are to be tried within the state where they occurred, without federal intervention.

Perhaps the most important of these rights was a reaffirmation of the limits of the power of the Constitution found in the Tenth Amendment, which states that all federal government rights not specifically set forth in the Constitution are reserved to the citizens and to the states.

Because the Constitution and the Bill of Rights have stood two hundred years of scrutiny, we are in danger of taking them for granted. Yet at the time they were enacted, there were no other laws on the face of the Earth that guaranteed such freedom to its citizens and checks on the power of a central government.

Often copied by other nations, but always with less substantial guarantees, the U.S. Constitution has withstood the test of time as a pragmatic, workable document that allows no one individual or no one branch of government enough power to endanger the continued welfare of the land.

WAR WITHOUT BULLETS

The Cold War

After the end of WW II, the U.S. engaged in another war, – a "Cold War" -- against the U.S.S.R.. This was a war fought not in the heat of battle, but it was a war nonetheless. Today, an extension of that original Cold War still goes on, even though the political consolidation of the enemy has been uprooted.

True, we all celebrated the destruction of the Berlin Wall, the overthrow of the Soviet government, and the re-nationalization of all the countries that had been unwillingly consolidated into the United Soviet Socialistic Republic.

But those events, however important in history, did not end the Cold War against the Soviet Union; America used means other than battle to drain the U.S.S.R. of its resources.

We had the money, the technology, and the commitment to maintain economic sanctions against the U.S.S.R., to continue a war of attrition to infiltrate the Soviet intelligence system, to build better weapons and to maintain the constant threat of military superiority should a battle take place.

After the United States used nuclear power against Japan in the closing months of World War II, no nation -- even the U.S.S.R. with its emphasis on building bigger and better weapons of destruction -- wanted to risk a nuclear attack. Both sides continued to build more destructive weapons but never used them.

The U.S.S.R. used all its resources to maintain military preparedness, while the U.S. -- far richer in resources and economic power -- allowed the U.S.S.R. to drain itself at the expense of its people's welfare over a period of forty years.

America could afford to wait out the eventual collapse of the Soviet government, occasionally prodding the process along by maintaining a display of its strength. Economic sanctions against the U.S.S.R. caused that nation's economy to falter.

The Soviet leadership saw the continued rise in America's economic strength while its own resources were all used to maintain it's military. Eventual collapse of the Soviet government was inevitable under those circumstances.

But the United States has not yet consolidated its winnings in the Cold War. It has not intervened to dictate the terms or the manner in which the successor governments of the former Soviet nations will conduct themselves in the future.

The Cold War is almost over. The U.S. always had an insurmountable advantage in this war-game. We have dictated such a pace in advancing our economy and our industrial power base that a communist system cannot possibly keep pace, and we effectively drove the U.S.S.R. into bankruptcy.

The U.S. could always up the ante to create more innovative weapons systems. President Reagan's Star Wars system was the proverbial last straw for the Soviet Union. Regardless of whether it worked, the U.S.S.R. had to assume it did, and trying to come up with a comparable system finally bank-rupted the Soviet Union, causing its economy to col-lapse.

It's Cleanup Time

Think about it for a moment and consider. A nu-clear war between the U.S. and the U.S.S.R. would have probably resulted in a holocaust wiping out most of the people and other living creatures and organisms on earth. For this reason, both countries tried to win by other means.

A war without bullets -- a "Cold War" -- be-came an instrument of confrontation between the U.S. and the U.S.S.R.. During this time the major fo-cus was on the information gathering apparatus on both sides to make sure that we knew what the other side was planning at any given moment in time and at any place on the globe.

The information gathering operations (spying agencies) naturally required the U.S. to deploy people and equipment all over the world in as close prox-imity to the U.S.S.R. and their bases of operations as possible.

To accomplish that aim, we had to deal with corrupt governments of rogue nations, using bribes, intimidation, or whatever else worked to make sure we were allowed to operate in their territory. (The lis-tening stations we established in Iran during that time are a good example.) Of course, the U.S.S.R. did the same, using Cuba and other countries for their bases.

In addition to information gathering, these cold war surrogates were also used to test and harass the other side in "theatrical battlefields." Tying up resources and attempting to create negative public opinion concerning the other side were regular "tools of the trade"; i.e., in Korea, Vietnam, Nicaragua, and Angola, among others.

Quite a big political and economic mess was created during the Cold War era. America now has an opportunity to clean up this mess and change its relationship with its old renegade allies against the Soviet Union.

The United States also has the opportunity and responsibility to help those nations to rid themselves of corrupt forces within their countries and help them to build a peaceful and prosperous free society.

Right vs. Wrong

It will take a few more years before the cleanup is done, and it may be argued that it was wrong and immoral to use those nations and people for our benefit. But think of it for a moment; the real beneficiary is all mankind on Earth.

The alternative was a possible nuclear war in which case those very same people and nations would have come out even worse -- first, because whoever survived the nuclear holocaust in the U.S. would be preoccupied with recovery and would have nothing extra available to offer in support to other people and nations. Second, missile defense systems would have probably redirected incoming missiles to the oceans or less populated areas. (i.e., if we intercepted a missile over Africa or the Middle East, the U.S. as well as the U.S.S.R. would have chosen to detonate the warheads there instead over our territory).

Nuclear War Must Be Avoided At Any Cost!

The Unites States was dragged into two World Wars in its short history. None of those wars were of our making, but we still ended up losing the lives of hundreds of thousands of our soldiers and carrying the economic burden of assisting our former enemies in rebuilding their societies.

Toward the end of World War II, nuclear energy was under development to be used as a potent weapon by Germany, Russia and the U.S.. We finished it first and successfully used atomic bombs to conclude that war. In the following forty years the U.S. and the U.S.S.R. were locked into a nuclear stand-off called the Cold War.

The U.S. prevailed in its effort to prevent a nuclear holocaust at an enormous cost. An unfortunate by-product of those Cold War years was the underground proliferation of nuclear devices which now might be in the hands of countries, dictators and terrorists who have a very different perspective on the value of human life.

The U.S. now has the burden of ensuring those weapons of mass destruction will be neutralized before any irresponsible country or irresponsible group has an opportunity to use them anywhere on Earth.

If that did happen, the result would be a devastating holocaust affecting the whole population of the Earth. The U.S. is the only country which has the power and the resources to declare war on any country or group which may attempt to light the fuse. It is a covert war, and we have no choice but to vigilantly pursue our objective for the sake of the human race.

Unfortunately, because of the stealthy nature of this war, most of the time the enemy can not be clearly identified and erroneous decisions will be made. However, in a situation like that we must err on the side of caution. We can not wait for the proverbial "smoking gun" because in this case it will be a huge "mushroom cloud."

Any price which we will incur during this fight will be significantly less than the alternative during a nuclear confrontation, in which we would end up being a participant again no matter where the event would begin.

Preempting the Enemy

While we are busy cleaning up the political landscape, we have to make it clear to the rest of the world that we won't tolerate any attempt by any country to "turn the clock back." America must pre-empt any effort to hinder our clean-up efforts.

The noted Prussian military theorist, Karl Von Clausewitz, said that "timidity causes a thousand times more damage than audacity." As the world's only remaining super power, we have a global responsibility to prevent other nations from actions harmful to both our own country and to others.

Until after World War II, the U.S. was noted for never firing the first shot -- of not attacking unless we were attacked first. But the days are over in which it was possible to wait for the proverbial "smoking gun" before defending ourselves suitably.

War now, with weapons of mass destruction, can potentially begin and end in minutes. Devastation can be global, not national. The luxury of waiting too long to disarm a conflict before it can begin is no longer affordable. America can no longer be a passive bystander in preventing world conflict.

With our superior information-gathering capabilities about potential destructive actions by other nations, we have an obligation to defend not only our own shores but also those of the other nations of the world.

Not responding to a threat when we know about it and have the capability to avert it would be a crime against humanity, and all nations will suffer the consequences of American inaction -- or benefit from America's action.

Are We Safe Yet?

Our way of life and our commitment to follow the law of the land has already proven costly. On September 11, 2001, America learned the hard way how our enemies can take advantage of our free and open society.

Despite the enormity of that event, the American people have allowed the government to institute only the kind of measures which won't impede our freedom and the laws of our land.

Following that tragedy, the people of the United States are doing something that comes naturally to them. They have changed their attitude and decidedly shifted their attention toward threats of any kind. No longer are Americans passive bystanders. We are now becoming proactively defensive. The expression "Let's roll!" from one of the heroes buried in the fields of Pennsylvania became a call for action.

Before 9-11, based on the past, the terrorists believed that we were passive and would not fight back. That's why when they hijacked the planes, they were confident enough to proceed with their plan with only ten people on their team and some box cutters with which to threaten passengers on board.

When the people on the third airplane learned that their own plane might be used by the terrorists as a bomb, they decided to resist and were able to foil the plan by sacrificing their lives.

The action of those people sent a message to future would-be terrorists and did more for our future security than probably any government-initiated plan and activity.

Free people are unpredictable, and they are the riskiest targets for any terrorist plan.

Weapon of Peace

Our most potent weapon in the effort to prevent war and to keep the peace continues to remain what it had been during the Cold War: information.

Timely intelligence helps us keep the peace or face and stop or even pre-empt a potential enemy before it can do damage to the world. The cutting edge of intelligence as a weapon is secrecy. Knowing what other nations are planning is one thing. Exposing what we know about their plans is quite another.

Managing the dissemination of information regarding what we know and how we found out about it is essential to continually gain effective intelligence on what another nation may be doing to build up military forces.

With secrecy in the intelligence community, we can choose the time and place and even the method to respond to the threat of a potential enemy. Using information wisely is the key to success.

Highly advanced technologies and potent satellite capabilities remain effective in monitoring activities of other nations on the ground. For years it has been widely publicized that America can see via satellite photos great detail of troop movements and deployment of naval forces at sea -- and we have even boasted about our ability to be able to read license plates and documents at ground level via satellite imagery.

While we tout our capabilities, we do not and should not as a nation broadcast what we learn.

Let's say, for example, that our satellite images were to reveal that a shipment of weapons of mass destruction was moving from Iraq to another country in order to conceal it from us. If we act "honestly" and disclose that information, it will force our hand and require us to act against that country even when the time and place are disadvantageous for us.

Disclosing that information would not benefit our objectives, but it would expose our capabilities.

We must maintain an effective balance between what we know and what we reveal, and we should only reveal what we must about our strength in intelligence gathering capabilities.

When the U.S. discloses the extent of its covert intelligence and what is known about weapons and potential global threats, our ability to deal with those threats before they become active is weakened. Disclosing this information prematurely also means that we disclose our technology for gathering this information. It is wiser to wait and choose our time to reveal what we know after the threat has been stopped.

Our own safety and that of other nations, our critics among them, may depend on our maintaining this balance between freedom of information and secrecy for protection.

Cold War Two is in Progress

Gullible leaders and citizens in other countries are easily lured into believing that America is bent on world domination and the imposition of our form of government on all other nations.

Why is this happening now? The Soviet Union collapsed a decade ago, and the newly formed Eastern European nations are now creating their own forms of government, not all of them modeled on the U.S., by any means.

During that time, the U.S. assisted other countries in achieving freedom from dictatorships but has not shown any inclination to force those nations into our own democratic mold or to extend our power abroad.

Yet this belief persists. For half a century, the United States and the Soviet Union were locked in a Cold War where each dared not use the nuclear arsenals at their disposal because each knew that the devastation would be global if they were to do so, destroying their own countries along with the rest of the world.

Each super power built up alliances with other countries to strengthen their own positions, offering favorable trade, armaments, loans, and many other "goodies" to attract allies.

Today, with only the United States in a position of real power, the industrialized nations of the world are concerned with our ultimate intentions and objectives. If they do not wish to align themselves with American strategy and political intentions, they have no place else to go for support and resources.

Friend vs. Friends

How did our former allies become our political foes? Political friendships always have a basis in national self-interest. Over two centuries ago, France aided the United States in its struggle for independence from Great Britain -- not so much because of a benevolent attitude and sympathy for the emerging republic, but far more so in order to engage Great Britain's forces and prevent the British from expanding their own empire.

In the more recent past, the United States supported Middle Eastern nations to keep the Soviet Union out of Afghanistan for similar reasons.

In today's global political climate, the primary reason behind most modern wars -- both "cold" and "hot" -- is economic survival.

Under Saddam Hussein, Iraq was a buyer of many goods that other nations produced -- France, Germany, and post-Soviet Russia all found a ready market for their goods in Iraq. Russia benefited greatly because their entire economy for more than forty years had been geared to producing military weapons -- no retooling needed, and their largely unemployed labor force could be put back to work.

The U.S. stepped in, first in the Gulf War and again in 2003, to destroy Iraq's dictatorship and allow the development of a new government controlled by its citizens. A major source of economic gain was lost to European nations with the collapse of Hussein's government, and resentment against the U.S. ran high.

Quite probably, given time to rebuild, Iraq will again be in a position to trade with other nations as it did in the past, although their focus will most likely be on goods and services for their citizens rather than on building an arsenal of weapons. At such a time, the European nations who benefited from trading with Iraq in the past will again see a favorable balance of payments.

This rebuilding will take years, however, because new governments traditionally lack the means to do business on a global scale. Until then, resentment of U.S. interference and the costly economic consequences will continue to engender an anti-American attitude from Iraq's former European trading partners who are losing a major market for their goods.

America's action in Iraq has generated suspicion that the U.S. might do the same elsewhere -- it's the European way of thinking, based on their history and economic strategy. The fact that historically America has always been uniquely generous to its former enemies in a post-war era does little to change this persistent belief -- and does little to help European nations to regain the lost income as a result of the fall of Hussein's regime.

Europe's focus is on immediate financial gain, and the U.S. is seen as a threat to that gain in Iraq and potentially elsewhere, so resentment against America continues to intensify.

Power Shift

As long as there were two world super powers aligned against each other, the remaining nations could generally conduct their affairs internally and in international trade without outside influence.

Both the U.S. and the Soviet Union were focused on each other, and the remaining national powers could benefit economically by aligning themselves with either super power.

When the Soviet Union collapsed, that left just one super power with the technology, wealth, and internal dynamics capable of dictating policy on a global scale -- and the U.S. as the remaining super power no longer needs to coax other nations into supporting our democratic aims by offering economic support.

As long as the Soviet Union and the United States were aligned against each other, ironic as it seems, this conflict created a comfortable situation for many other countries, knowing they had substantial support for their own territories and economies while the U.S. and the Soviet Union competed to gain their support.

Now the Soviet Union is gone, and the U.S. no longer needs those strategic alignments for military or economic purposes. Instead, the U.S. has focused its foreign policy -- and its foreign aid -- on assisting emerging third-world democracies and on freeing other countries from dictatorships so they can determine their own political destinies.

This new situation has created resentment among the industrialized nations, especially in Western Europe. The competition for their support has vanished -- and so, too, have many of the "incentives" -- i.e., foreign aid -- that was so readily available a decade ago. Add to that the indirect interference the U.S. is causing by taking an aggressive stance against oppressive dictatorships, which also has aroused the ire of many nations.

While Western European nations have not viewed dictatorships as desirable forms of government, they have, nevertheless, traded with them for economic gain. Many of the former Soviet member nations are still desperately trying to build their economies, and they have benefited from selling their arsenals to Middle Eastern despots. However, once the U.S. intervened in Iraq (and shows signs of doing so in other rogue nations to protect American citizens), all the countries that traded with Iraq suddenly found their highly profitable market shut off.

Thus, Cold War II has been declared on us in covert ways and is in progress now.

The balance of power among the nations has been upset. This time, the new Cold War is being fought stealthily by other industrialized nations against the United States by pitting the U.S. against traditionally unstable, hostile nations in the Middle East and Asia.

What they have yet to realize is that they have already lost this Cold War because America has the resources to deploy on many fronts -- both economic and military.

One of the great fears of many nations is that when going up against a power as formidable as the United States, they will lose their cultural identity and become part of the American way of life, where everyone shops at Wal-Mart, eats at McDonald's and KFC, and drives General Motors cars. To be fair, there is some evidence that America is making global economic inroads by introducing American products, foods, and transportation everywhere. General Motors is building plants in China and Mexico. In countries around the world, the familiar "Golden Arches" of McDonald's loom everywhere.

We are exporting American products around the globe. But our economy is by no means a one-way street. If you were to check the label in your sneakers, you will probably find that it says "Made in China." The tag on your Hanes tee-shirt may say "Made in Honduras," and the shirt you wear might say "Made in Mexico."

Our computer components come from China, Japan, and Thailand, and we outsource the tech support to keep them running to India and the Philippines, and soon IBM laptop computers will be made in China through a new international consortium jointly owned by IBM and Chinese nationals.

The truth is that American discount chains keep prices down for U.S. consumers by importing as much as our manufacturers export, and America and its trading partners all prosper from this interchange of goods.

Unfortunately, the nations that do not want to adhere to American trading standards -- including protection for human rights and fair employment conditions – are finding themselves at a severe disadvantage in world markets. If they don't play by our rules, they don't play at all. What these countries fail to realize is that trade partnerships do not equate with a political takeover by the U.S., so their fear of our country's power continues to escalate. They hate what America represents: the strongest political power in the world, which cannot be conquered or deterred.

The Power of One

There is nothing we can do about the attitude of other nations at the present time but continue on our present path. Why? The hatred of other nations, many of them our professed allies in times past, is based on fear of American power they cannot influence or control.

When an attitude is based on emotion rather than logic, there is no effective way to counter it, except to allow a great deal of time to elapse, so that the current attitudes will gradually be replaced through positive experience by acceptance of our benevolent aim of peace and freedom for all nations.

However, a change in attitude is not a matter of sudden recognition but rather a gradual evolutionary shift over generations. For now, weaker nations will continue to dislike the strongest one which imposes standards of conduct on them. Yet if no one speaks out for freedom across the globe, oppression will grow. And if we do not speak out, who will? Who can do so successfully apart from the United States?

If nations that seek freedom have nowhere to turn, what will happen to them over time? As the only remaining super power, America is the only nation that can fill this role.

For the first time since the days of the Roman Empire, there is just one nation that is not merely a regional super power but is the only global super power with the economic and military power to be the guardian of freedom everywhere.

Historical Roots of Current Attitudes

European nations are basing their current attitudes on negative experience with their own strong governments in the past -- none of which were truly democratic in nature.

In Europe, countries both large and small were for many centuries under the control of absolute monarchies, dictatorships, and tyrants.

Their parliaments tended to be weak and ineffectual and always at the mercy of a ruler who could disband any group that threatened the ruler's power. European experience with real democracy is quite recent, and they are patterning their 'democratic' government forms on their own history, fearful of putting too much power in the hands of the people and private enterprise.

True democracy is frightening to any country with a long history of strong, often despotic leadership. Sadly, these countries see America as a global tyrant -- and for many nations, it's the only form of government they have experienced over the centuries, so they cannot grasp what real democracy is like.

They find it difficult to accept the American concept of a government that has only the powers given to it by the people in contrast to their own past governments which gave the people very limited power.

For now, other nations oppose the U.S. in almost all our international actions because they see no other way to stop us from gaining power over them -- that they are wrong in their belief that we seek world domination will only be changed over generations. For now, they judge American aims by their own past experience, fearing that we will take over their nations if we have the opportunity and resources.

Of course, we do have the means to affect world control, but we have never done so and it is not our desire to do so in the future.

Quite probably, there will be a day in the far future when there is a single world government, but the form of such a government and its structure are still unknown. The day when all nations will be united under one banner is too distant for us to consider in this post-Soviet era where new nations are struggling with their own new national identities.

Opposition to America can be expected to continue in the decades ahead because accepting the fact that there is no way to win "Cold War II" is unthinkable. While we know our intentions are simply for world peace, not through domination but through a free world citizenry, only the passage of time will allow other countries to accept this fact.

The Last Super Power

Some day, other major world powers will emerge as strong unions where there is mutual agreement on common goals and principles. Meanwhile, America will still be evolving, moving ahead in technology, encouraging other nations to seek freedom and peace, while maintaining our own economic and military supremacy.

The simple truth is that we are so far ahead, it is impossible for current national governments – even for a future cohesive European Union – to catch up to the U.S. in the foreseeable future.

Future Wars

The outcome has already been decided and the only nation in the world today that has a sufficient depth of resources to win any and all wars, however long they may last, is the United States of America. Only our nation has shown its ability to incur the cost of any war. In both technology and natural resources, America has no match in the world today.

Even as third-world nations gain economic strength, America will remain ahead because the U.S. is a free democracy which can continue to grow at a faster rate than any other society.

We are the only nation with the ability to pay the cost of winning -- whether that victory requires fighting a series of battles, or waging a war of attrition through economic sanctions and the threat of military force. Thus, the United States has already won all past and future wars!

CHAPTER TWO
"L'Enfant Terrible?"

Growing Pains

We are not a "terrible baby," but the world may see us that way and this baby has to work to change that perception. Sometimes we need to remind ourselves that our country is still just a toddler in the eyes of history. We are still acting a bit clumsy, still somewhat unsophisticated, and still very naïve about the history and the affairs of the rest of the world.

The United States is the new kid on the world's –playground-- and many times we act like a child, uncomfortable with our size and power, feeling guilty when we hurt others in self defense, even when they were the ones who played rough.

Our country is infinitely generous and friendly toward others but also impatient and has a very short attention span.

We became the strongest nation and the leader of the free world by default and we can't delegate this role to others. Consequently we must accept, albeit reluctantly, our inherent duty to keep peace and order among our – playmates --.

Our Place in World Society

Although we Americans are justly proud of two hundred plus years of history as a nation, in the eyes of the rest of the world we are still at the beginning of a social experiment in democracy.

America is regarded by other nations as little more than an infant in terms of its age as a nation. Even though the U.S. has proved itself to be superior to much older nations in economic strength, political power, and technology, those countries whose roots go back almost two millennia tend to view the U.S. as somewhat like a giant toddler on steroids -- strong and powerful, but inexperienced and naïve in its approach to world politics.

Well into the twentieth century, America went along like a giant baby, toddling along happily and peacefully, focused far more on its own growth than on being part of a global political structure. And like most young children, America lacked some of the wisdom that comes with maturity and longevity.

What makes America so different from other nations -- and why has the American great experiment prevailed when other powers in the past who tried some form of a republic failed?

There are many causes for America's successful growth into the leading world power. The United States is not the first political power to have a republic with a representative government -- but it is the first to succeed so far in modern times! To nurture our success, we need to understand the critical differences in the American experience from those that went before.

Democracy & Freedom

We must understand that democracy and freedom are not a natural state for humanity. Throughout history people have led by the strongest person in power and told what to do. When it became unbearable, people fought back and started all over in much the same way, leading to the same results after a while. It is always too easy and comfortable to blame somebody else for existing problems.

To be free and to be responsible in one's choices is very difficult and unsettling for many people. Change is also hard and disruptive to the people's lives. It is very much human nature to try to fix what we have already rather than to start all over, especially where the outcome is unknown.

The U.S. is a very unique place because people here are born into freedom or came to this country because they desired to live in a free society.

Leader-Dependent Societies

Long before America was discovered, Rome overthrew its last monarch and instituted a prototype of a republican form of government that lasted almost 500 years, from 509 BC to 42 BCE. After ousting its last king, the Romans decided on a government led by two consuls who would have absolute joint authority but for whom there would be checks and balances in their power.

The consuls were each elected to a one-year term by an assembly. However, each consul could veto the decisions of the other. The Roman Senate, whose members were appointed for life from among Rome's aristocracy, could appoint a dictator who would have absolute authority for up to six months during a time of threat of invasion or other political crisis.

Thus, there were checks and balances on individual power in the Roman Republic, similar to but nowhere nearly as extensive as those of a modern democratic republic. The limited term of each consul meant that he could not accomplish much meaningful change in the Republic in a one-year term.

Over time the Roman Republic began to shift its methods of government. Plebeians, the working class, began to insist on representation, eventually winning the right to form its own assembly and to pass decrees -- but these decrees were only binding on other plebeians, not on the aristocracy.

Rome's great experiment in a republic ended after a long period of internal civil war. The Republic was abandoned, and an emperor was chosen following the deaths of three prominent Romans who had seized power and established a triumvirate. Ironically, these three men -- Cassius, Pompey, and Julius Caesar -- had been strong protectors of a republican form of government before taking power. It was Caesar's nephew, Augustus, who became Rome's first emperor.

Although Rome's republic ultimately failed due to corrupt power mongers within, it lasted almost half a millennium before collapsing -- over twice as long as the U.S. has existed. Rome's ensuing Empire lasted almost another 500 years before being invaded successfully by foreign powers.

Along the way, numerous emperors were assassinated and many corrupt imperial government officials contributed mightily to the final fall of the Roman Empire. Rome had expanded successfully during its Republic, and in the next 200 years under a succession of emperors, Rome was able to establish and hold its many provinces and conquered territories, enforcing its law on the Mediterranean world -- the famous *Pax Romana* -- the Roman Peace -- was maintained by Rome's legions and provincial governors for two centuries until the Empire began to collapse from corruption within.

There were no checks and balances on the imperial power of the emperors. Yet Rome prospered during those centuries, building new roads, bringing an abundant water supply to the city of Rome, and a thriving government led by a system of laws that applied to all its citizens. However, after a series of corrupt emperors and a gradual decline in the power of the Roman Senate, the system collapsed. What has began as a republic, deteriorated into a chaotic government without real, cohesive power by the end of the Imperial period.

What Rome's government lacked that the U.S. has is a series of Constitutional checks and balances on each branch so that the entire government of the U.S. is subject to Constitutional constraints on power. The republics of the past and many empires that developed a republican approach to their governments failed for two reasons:

- First, they were *leader dependent,* instead of relying on a system of government that provided the checks and balances which would ensure that no one person could do any real damage to the system. This balanced form of government is what the U.S. has today.
- Second, they built their nations on *conquest* of other lands instead of liberating those lands from despots and tyrants as the U.S. is now doing throughout the world.

When Alexander the Great set about conquering other countries around the Mediterranean, he established governors of those territories to act independently while reporting to him. Yet those new national authorities were still dependent on a strong leader for their success. As soon as a leader failed or died, the government collapsed.

Without a strong leader in command and without a structure that was not dependent on one individual to dictate orders, the country soon fell back into its old system and found another leader to be in control. The fate of the country was dependent not on a system of laws, but rather on the whims of a single individual.

Attila the Hun also expanded his territory by conquest. Yet as soon as he died, the Tatars who had followed him could not hold his expanded territories together. The Republic of Rome failed with Julius Caesar's death and chose an emperor, with increasingly disastrous results over the Republic's remaining lifetime. Even the famous *Lex-Romana*, the code of Roman law which guaranteed rights to citizens, was often swept aside when an emperor had a score to settle with those under his rule.

The overthrow of the Tsar in Russia and the forming of the U.S.S.R. under Lenin also ended in disaster with Lenin's death. The ensuing regimes all concentrated their resources on building a militaristic government bent on seizing new territories to add to the Soviet Union -- and those leaders held absolute power.

The French philosopher Voltaire's statement that "power corrupts, and absolute power corrupts absolutely" has been seen throughout the world in every nation where a monarch, a tsar, a dictator, or a despot has assumed power.

Leader Neutral Democracy

Contrast these earlier governments and failed republics with that of the U.S., which is leader neutral. We have had over the past two century's presidents of every sort. Some were enlightened progressive leaders. Some were ill-equipped for the job to which they were elected. Many rose to become revered for their contributions to the nation.

The occupations of our former U.S. presidents include that of movie star (Ronald Reagan), peanut farmer (Jimmy Carter), former generals (Andrew Jackson, Ulysses S. Grant, Dwight D. Eisenhower) and haberdasher (Harry Truman), and a host of others.

The records of American presidents are as varied as their occupations. Many made a permanent record worthy of tribute, particularly those who held the office during difficult times of war. Others were far less successful.

Yet they all had something in common: They were bound by Constitutional law, which allowed Congress, with its direct representation of the people, to pass laws even over a presidential veto. Congress also has the power to impeach a president who discredits his office, or to force a president to resign through the threat of impeachment, as in the case of Richard Nixon.

The bottom line is that no one authority figure in the U.S. can ever seize power and overturn the laws of the land set forth in the Constitution. The U.S. government is not leader dependent, but rather it is *leader neutral*. The United States is a leader neutral society where no one person has absolute power!

This inherent bias in favor of law, not leaders, has played a major role in our foreign policy. We are willing to intervene in world affairs for our own protection or to right injustices and prevent continued tyranny in other countries. We are willing to spread freedom to other countries instead of conquering them and imposing our will on them.

When America has stepped in during recent decades to aid another country, one of its first actions after restoring peace is to work with that nation to establish its own government and free elections rather than annexing it, as was the practice among leader dependent nations in the past. Laws, not leaders, make for enduring freedom.

America's Success

Is it a great experiment or a lasting legacy? For some of our critics, the jury is still out, and the United States has yet to withstand the test of time as older nation's measure longevity.

For Americans today, democracy is unquestionably a success -- not perfect by any means, but far better than all other forms of government throughout the world.

Our power is based on our form of democracy, freedom for our citizens and an underlying foundation of Constitutional law allowing the promotion of democracy but not accommodating colonialism.

The American Cradle
the Nurturing Land

The physical environment of the infant American Republic played a vital role in its early success as a nation. Transportation between America and its neighbors in Europe took months, not the few hours of flight time today.

That made it an unattractive target for a potential invasion, as the British discovered when trying to reclaim its errant colonies. And in the peace that followed the American Revolution and the War of 1812, America was left with broad, unexplored frontiers and a vast natural landscape to expand and grow as no other nation could.

We had in our first century what Germany sought unsuccessfully in World War II -- *lebensraum* -- living room, for people to stake out a claim to homesteads, to build towns and factories and a network of continental transport on rivers and later by rail, to expand between two protective oceans that limited the ability of others to interfere with the growth of the new nation.

In this period, new technology was born, businesses thrived, and America began to take its place in the councils of the world, not as a weak emerging power but as a strong and vital presence, unconquerable by any invading force.

The lack of speedy global communication, the distance across oceans, and the lack of any weapon system sophisticated enough to touch American shores gave the nation room for growth and development on an unprecedented scale.

Constitutional Protection

Even at the most critical moment in American history, when internal strife threatened to tear apart the emerging republic, America did possess a "secret weapon" to ensure its continued existence. The bold document of the Constitution envisioned by our founding fathers gave a legal framework for a government that could endure even the challenge of a threatened division within the country.

Before the Civil War, in many respects the states that formed the union thought of themselves as separate, united by a common federal government, but still in many ways unique and individual powers.

To have a common currency was an indisputable asset.

To have a central government to negotiate treaties and make trading policies was good, but many of the states still thought of themselves as separate powers with loose allegiance to the central core values of a single political entity.

When the Civil War was over, it was well settled that the bonds that united the individual states were inseparable.

A historian once noted in studying American writings before the Civil War that statements in print about the country often used a plural verb, referring to the States as "The United States are..." After the Civil War, the usage changed in writing to "The United States is..." We were one unit, indivisible, a single political and social entity in our own eyes and in the eyes of the world.

Where "The Great Experiment" Stands Today

In the beginning of this chapter, America was compared to a giant toddler on steroids -- still an infant in the eyes of far older nations.

During most of the two centuries since the founding of the United States, European nations were largely occupied with their own affairs and internal struggles, and for a long time failed to recognize just how powerful the United States was becoming, except for a few times when the young nation flexed its political and military muscle in world affairs.

Indeed, until the early part of the twentieth century, America was in some ways isolationist both by its own desire and by political design, and it was easy for other countries to underestimate America's growing strength until its entry into World War II. After that war, no other nation could seriously challenge America's power and hope to survive.

The United States has a long history of using its power with benevolence, aiding other nations who had been enemies -- not to seize them and impose its will through territorial expansion but rather to help those nations grow and stabilize with continued U.S. aid.

However, to think that America's close allies and even emerging nations who are heavily dependent on U.S. support are grateful and pleased would be politically and socially naïve. Their very dependence on the U.S. inevitably breeds resentment stemming from their fear that if that assistance were to be cut off, their survival would be threatened.

The newly emerging nations, principally the former members of the Soviet Union, face a greater challenge. Technology today provides instant communication. People all around the globe can see via television and hear via radio how well the citizens of the United States live.

These nations have overthrown a dictatorship and now want not only democracy but also instant access to the "good life" enjoyed by other countries -- but first and foremost, by the U.S. itself, which illustrates the very best in the good life that emerging nations cannot hope to achieve for decades to come.

They must come to realize that what America is today was the result of a unique set of circumstances that can only be replicated -- to a limited degree -- by a long struggle and internal building over time.

At some point if these new nations fail to realize their version of the American dream, they may opt for the security of the old ways where decisions were made for them under a dictatorship which gave them limited freedom but a form of security where the government provided control. They have had a taste of freedom but do not yet understand that freedom imposes individual responsibility for success or failure. For now, they only see that success still eludes them.

These new nations stand at a critical juncture in their history. They can begin to embrace the responsibility that comes with freedom and democracy or fall back into the false security of a leadership that makes their decisions for them.

They can build strong constitutional democracies founded in a body of law or opt for a dictatorship that chooses for them. In this critical period, the role America plays in guiding these nations forward will determine just how far America can extend its great experiment on a global scale.

We Must Be Patient

While we are on our quest to spread democracy we must be patient and look back at our own history and see how long it took for us to form and shape and nurture our society to become what it is today. We must resist temptation to view the world's unfolding events with a "soap opera" mentality.

Nothing will be over in an hour, or even a year or two. Freedom is not free. It may cost a lot, and we have to pay a price to maintain our freedom. We can't afford to become bored with the effort and just walk away!

As our society moves forward and promotes our way of life, we must recognize and come to terms with the fact that other nations' cultural traditions will affect their views and attitudes toward everything they do when adopting a democratic form of government.

In some societies, the people believe that they have no power to control their destiny but are controlled by it. In general, they may be closed to outside influences and think in more subjective terms. Their feelings and their traditional values influence their decisions.

Some societies suppress individuality, and people work closely in whatever group to which they are loyal, striving more for group consensus than individual action.

A person's age and position in many society's hierarchy is revered, and the view and the decisions of the group's elders are followed without question. Many societies are not tolerant towards deviant behavior and harbor strong biases against outsiders, based on centuries of their own history.

Their values and methods to distinguish right from wrong and good from evil are usually based on

they religious commitments and centuries of historical precedents. People in some cultures may not accept facts as the source of truth.

To acknowledge these differences will help us
to reduce our anxiety over the slow progress of our
efforts and allow us to be gentler and more understanding about the enormity of the task we are under-
taking.

CHAPTER THREE
Wherever We Are – There We Are

Politics on Our Mind

Our current state of affairs is the result of the sum of all our decisions made in the past as citizens of this nation as expressed through our democratic voting process!

At any given time our government and its actions directly reflect the views and values of the majority of our society!

Politicians are chameleons by nature. They always tell us what we want to hear and not what we need to know.

Our Government Is Us

Two centuries ago, Americans set out to establish a new government, "to form a more perfect union," in the words of the Declaration of Independence. And that document begins with a phrase that should remind all of us that we *are* the government: *"We the people..."*

The union that was formed was the result of the people acting in concert and was the genesis of the representative government we enjoy today, but our government is only representative of our choice if we actually make a choice!

The fact is that *the government is us!* It's not some faceless bunch of people running amok in Washington with our hard-earned tax dollars. It's *"We the people"* in action! Our government has always been a decision-making body that reflects the will of the people who elected it.

If we did not choose to cast a vote in favor of a candidate, if we did not seek to understand the issues and the platforms of each candidate so we could make an informed decision on Election Day -- we chose to let someone else cast a ballot for us and pick our leaders without any protest by us. So why should we complain if the results we get aren't the results we want?

Perhaps it would be more to the point if we were to complain about the decisions made by those who chose to vote instead complaining about the leaders they elected. After all, if we didn't vote, we let those who did choose for us. Or we could go one step further and not allow people to criticize our government unless they have voted, thereby earning the right to voice an opinion.

The irony is that by maintaining our democratic form of government, those who vote reaffirm the right of all citizens -- those who voted and those who didn't -- to voice an opinion about government policies and practices through the First Amendment right of free speech.

Ultimately, for our government to be the best it can be, we must all take responsibility for choosing

effective leaders because we have the most to gain --
or lose -- by the choices we make.

We have to live with the results of every election until the next one roll around and a lot we don't
like can happen between elections.

One Vote

Democratic governments represent the views and
values of society as a whole, or more specifically, the views and values of that segment of society
that makes its wishes known. The form of government we have in the United States today is the result
of the past decisions made by the majority of the
people who vote and who express their concerns and
wishes to their elected representatives in Congress.

The result is that instead of having the will of
the people as a whole reflected in the decisions made
by Congress and the laws enacted by that body, we
have a government by an increasingly vocal minority
-- those individuals who choose to vote in our elections and to express their views to the government on
an ongoing basis.

The past fifty years has shown a decline in the
number of people who vote in every national and
state election. Today only a minority of those eligible
to vote do so. If you don't participate in the electoral
process, you have, in effect, allowed those who vote
to make your decisions for you. The excuses nonvoters make are many:

- "I can't take time away from work..."
- "I don't like either of the candidates..."
- "I forgot to register..."
- "My one vote won't really make a difference among so many others..."

One vote does make a difference. In 1920, the Nineteenth Amendment was presented to Congress -- the Amendment that gave women the right to vote -- and one vote by a Tennessee Congressional Representative, Harry Burn tipped the balance in favor of passing the Amendment. Our history is filled with examples where one vote made all the difference:

- In 1776, one vote gave America the English language instead of German.
- In 1839, one vote elected Marcus Morton Governor of Massachusetts.
- In 1845, one vote brought Texas into the Union.
- In 1868, one vote saved President Andrew Johnson from impeachment.
- In 1876, one vote gave Rutherford B. Hayes the Presidency of the United States.
- In 1941, one vote saved the Selective Service System just 12 weeks before Pearl Harbor.
- In 1960, John F. Kennedy was elected president by the narrowest of margins – one vote per precinct made the difference.

Historically, one vote has made a difference in the course of world events in places other than America. Imagine what the world political map and the events of the last few centuries would have been had these historic votes had shifted:

- In 1645, one vote gave Oliver Cromwell control of England.
- In 1649, one vote caused Charles I of England to be executed.
- In 1876, one vote changed France from a monarchy to a republic.
- In 1923, one vote gave Adolph Hitler leadership of the Nazi Party.
- One vote in each of these instances made a difference in the fate of kings and dictators. And in each case, one group of people -- the winners of the election -- dictated the fate of all the citizens of a country and ultimately the fate of many nations.

One vote ..... The gift our forefathers won for us in a long and bitter war and preserved for us in the Constitution of the United States is a gift to be cherished and protected and used by each of us.

Our vote is our personal testament to the value of the individual in society and to the values of that society as a whole. One vote is our affirmation of the gift our founding fathers gave us. One vote is our personal choice in democracy -- and it may well be that our one vote will safeguard our democracy in the years ahead.

If you choose not to vote, then you have effectively given others the right to make your choices for you. And if you don't like the election results, it's time to start thinking about how costly your choice not to vote has become to you. Only about half the eligible voters in America cast their ballots in elections.

The obvious conclusion to be drawn is that the other half of America is willing to accept the decisions made by others about their future, their economic well-being, their jobs, their healthcare, and their taxes.

When this country was new, it was considered both a privilege and a responsibility to vote in each election. The American Revolution had been fought to gain the privilege of the people deciding on the leaders who would guide the destiny of our country.

The people walked for miles or rode on horseback to a polling place where they could exercise their right as citizens to select their local, state, and federal representatives. They believed their votes counted -- and with each vote cast, they reaffirmed democracy as a system of government by the people.

Today in almost every conversation that turns to politics, the government is spoken of as an entity that is out there somewhere with a life of its own:

- "...the *Government* raised taxes"
- "...I don't like what the *Government* is doing these days"

- "...Why doesn't the *Government* fund a new healthcare system?"
- "...The *Government* interferes in local affairs too much."

The list of criticisms is endless, but they all have one thing in common. The speakers regard "the Government" as independent life form with a will of its own, embodied in a group of politicians who act independently of the desires or wishes of the voters.

Our personal involvement begins with voting, but it doesn't end there. It requires working for the best candidates for office, taking the time to really understand the issues confronting the nation, and playing an active role in giving any politician who doesn't perform his marching papers and sending him home.

We each have an opportunity to create change in the political process and in the fate of our nation, but we must exercise that right consistently to keep our country's democracy secure.

The Price of Freedom

The freedom we enjoy today was dearly bought by the sacrifices of our founding fathers when, in the words of the Declaration of Independence, they pledged their "lives, their fortunes, and their sacred honor" so that we would have the right to choose our leaders and decide how our country would be run. Today that right to choose our leadership, which we so often take for granted, is a freedom with a remarkably low price tag. Just one vote by each of us can tip the scales between war and peace, between prosperity and poverty, between a secure future or one that is filled with chaos and despair.

If we are not willing to pay that price, we leave to others the choices that affect us and our children in the years ahead. The choices we make today will determine the way we will live in the future.

In many cases, those choices we make through the electoral process and through voicing our opinions to our leaders will result in new laws being passed that will affect our health, our retirement income, our opportunities for jobs and education.

However if we fail to vote and make our wishes known, that means that we accept whatever choices our officials make without our input.

We Reap What We Sow

If we sow nothing, we may have a sorry harvest indeed, based on the decisions made by others which affect our personal well-being. The original price tag paid for freedom in this country was high. Many of our founding fathers lost everything as the result of the devastation caused by British troops during the Revolution.

Many of them died impoverished -- but probably none of them ever regretted the choice they made --- it was their choice to take a stand for a government of the people that made our own choices possible.

America is not the only nation that has taken a costly stand for liberty. In the closing years of the twentieth century, the people of Russia finally over-turned the Soviet leadership, and they are still finding that stand costly today as their recent elections bear out.

In Iraq, the first free election was held under threats of terrorist bombings and loss of life -- and those events did occur, but the people courageously came to the polls anyway. In new democracies all over the world, people are risking their lives to make their one vote count.

Our Politicians

Every four years we have an opportunity to make a major change in our national leadership and the direction our country is going — or we can choose to endorse the way our country is being run through re-electing our politicians already in office or someone else with a similar political agenda if that person is leaving.

But as soon as the election is over, we rapidly change from a nation of voters to a nation of arm-chair critics, with a great fondness for grumbling about the election results. Often we hear (or even make) comments like these.

- "Why doesn't the President solve this problem with imports as he promised to in his cam-paign?"
- "How can my Congressional Representative vote to raise taxes when he promised not to?"

- "What was my Senator thinking of when he voted for this energy bill after campaigning against it?"
- "What happened to all those campaign promises my Congressional Representative made?"

We elected our politicians based on the promises they made while on the campaign trail, so what went wrong? Didn't they mean what they said?

Politicians are wonderfully facile individuals, who are born chameleons by nature, ready to tell us what we want to hear but not necessarily what we need to know.

Their careers depend on favorable public opinion which gets them elected and re-elected, so they frequently offer simple solutions to complex problems because it plays well with the voters. Their goal is to look like they have the answers to our problems, and their political opponents do not. Being the one with all the easy answers is a major step forward in getting elected.

On the campaign trail, our politicians face a great temptation to address only those issues which are "hot buttons" at the moment with voters, regardless of whether those issues are the most important ones facing our country.

In fact, speaking up about the state of our country as a whole and what really needs to be done to keep the nation strong and safe could actually lose the election. So what's a politician to do? Many take the somewhat cynical view that they can't address real, but unpopular, issues and hope to get elected and without being elected, their opportunity to create any positive change will never occur. So they tell us what we want to hear:

- "I will hold the line on tax increases."
- "I will fight for better schools for our children."
- "I will work to stop the export of jobs from American shores.

Do any of the above statements sound familiar? They should -- all of them were popular campaign promises in the 2004 election -- and in many of the elections that went before. The tune may change with whatever *crisis du jour* is facing America at the moment, but the song remains the same.

Every election year, each politician makes campaign promises, and we vote for the person who promises us what we want. After the election is over and taxes go up, the new schools fail to materialize, and yet another company outsources its manufacturing to a third-world nation where wages are cheaper, we complain mightily about the politician we elected.

What if...?

What if, just once, the politician who is soliciting our votes tells us not what we want to hear but rather what we really need to know? What if a politician says?

"Lower taxes would be wonderful, but the cost of delivering all the services you demand is beyond the scope of our present budget. To keep delivering what you want takes more money and that means a tax increase because the taxes you pay now just aren't enough."

Or...

"Sure we want better schools for our children, but that will take a massive infusion of capital to build better schools, to hire more teachers, and to buy more state-of-the-art technology and books. Are you willing to pay for that?"

Or...

"Of course we want jobs for every American right here at home. But we live in a global economy, where companies can't deliver the goods you want at a price you're willing to pay with the present cost of American labor. Going offshore means companies can produce the car you buy or the clothes you wear at lower prices. Are you willing to pay more for these things to be made only in America?"

That's not what we want to hear from our politicians. The truth is not always popular with voters. We don't want to hear their honest answers to complex issues -- we want whatever problem confronts us to have an easy solution, and one that's not too painful for us to accept. So we vote for the politician who tells us what we want to hear, who reassures us that all will be well if elect him or her.

What We Need to Know

Each elected politician is the product of our choice. And by our willingness only to hear magical solutions to our country's problems, we are deluding ourselves by not confronting the real issues -- and telling our politicians to address those issues honestly.

The issues we face today require complex solutions. The truth is that these problems don't have simple answers. We should be asking our politicians to give us insight into the long-term solutions that are required in an economy that is no longer national, but global.

When we gripe about taxes and job exports, we need to look at the reality of the problems that our politicians do not discuss for fear of losing the election. The truth is that exporting jobs helps our own economy by providing cheaper goods and services today -- and it will help us in the future by making other countries self-sustaining with our present aid. The tax dollars we spend now will keep us from having to continue to support other nations in the future.

We need to know that supporting our fight to end tyranny in other nations really helps keep democracy safe for us. We need to know that the price of failing to do this could lead to other nations falling into dictatorships which could one day cause us to be surrounded by enemies.

We need to know that taxes are a very low price to pay for all the services we enjoy -- and that they support the Armed Forces who are keeping our country safe so we can enjoy the good life. These are not popular things for our politicians to tell us. It is not what we want to hear. But it is, indeed, what we need to know, so the choice is ours.

We can elect politicians with the easy answers or the ones who will honestly tell us what we need to know to continue to enjoy our freedom and prosperity.

CHAPTER FOUR
Our Influence

The Nucleus

The United States has become the hub of the world economy. We are now interdependent with all the nations of the world! The U.S. is the single most powerful nation on the face of the earth and now controls the safety and the welfare of the entire world!

We are not living under a protective "bubble" any longer. Every political decision we make has far-reaching global consequences!

Thinking in a Bubble

For the first decades of its existence, the United States existed relatively free from foreign influence. Time and distance allowed the infant republic to develop internally. Essentially, apart from trade, the United States kept to itself, even though wars were being fought in other parts of the world.

We tried to maintain this isolation during the early years of World War I, and again immediately before World War II. America's political stance towards its allies before entry into both these wars was essentially this: we will send supplies, even armaments, but it's not our war. Leave us out of it. In 1941, the attack on Pearl Harbor by the Japanese made it impossible for America to remain aloof from the conflict and the political concerns that emerged in the wake of that war during a very uneasy peace. Hence, the Cold War began. America soon was no longer the only nation with nuclear arms, superior armed forces, and worldwide intelligence organizations.

Yet with all these events and a constant escalation of the arms race, in some ways, American citizens have remained in a bubble. This is our homeland, isolated by distance from any potentially hostile nations.

Our own economy is strong. Even after the terrorist attacks on September 11, 2001, the majority of Americans still take the view that our nation is independent of other influences and continue to maintain the attitude of "America for Americans," without paying close attention to global events.

The Globalization of
American Interests

Today the U.S. is a global power, operating in a worldwide arena. The truth is that the welfare of the United States no longer rests solely on its own shores and its own resources. The welfare of this country is now inextricably linked to the welfare of the other nations of the world.

Whether we like it or not, when other nations are in trouble and suffer war, tyranny, natural disasters or man-made ones, America is affected, too. They call on the United States for help in any crisis, whether it's driving out a dictator, alleviating famine, or providing medical resources to fight the growing third-world AIDS epidemic. As the most powerful and the richest nation on Earth, we always respond, and our response affects our own economy.

When a third-world country suffers drought and famine and we send food supplies, we must pay the cost of donating those resources.

When our companies become involved in establishing manufacturing facilities in nations with a plentiful, cheap labor supply, our own employment rates are affected.

When we are able to buy goods and services cheaper because they are manufactured outside the U.S., we are pleased with the prices -- and if one of those products must then be returned to America for final assembly, the price goes up.

Our concerns -- both personal and political -- have become global, not merely national.

When America Sneezes...

However the reverse is also true. When the United States takes a political stand on any situation, be it the elimination of world hunger or the development of a new democracy, the other nations of the world are affected by those actions.

The saying holds true that "when America sneezes, all other nations catch cold." America's ability to impact the fate of all the other countries in the world is unparalleled in history, and our power on the world stage is unique.

The United States is not only a part of a global economy and a political nexus but also it is the leader that influences global events and politics. The U.S. is in this position by default. There is no other country capable of assuming world leadership. It is not a status that America deliberately chose, but it is a role that our nation must now play for our own survival and that of other nations.

Because the entire global economy is now interwoven, we can't decline to play the role we have been given.

The Globalization of Commerce

Go take a look in your closet, check the labels on your clothing and shoes. How many products do you see that say "Made in the USA"? Chances are good that there are only a few. Most clothing will have labels saying "Made in India, Made in Indonesia, and Made in the Philippines, Made in Japan"or"Made in China." Like this country, most of our wardrobes are global.

The next time you buy new auto parts for your car, you'll find that many of them are not from the U.S. but were made around the world. And when you see parts available that are made in America, there's a good chance that the American-made part will be more costly than its foreign-made duplicate.

This globalization of commerce has interwoven the American economy with that of other countries around the world, and those newly industrialized nations are benefiting greatly from the opportunity to sell their goods to U.S. customers.

We are converting our welfare dollars formerly given as a handout to other countries into trade dollars based on the labor pool of that country, which is leading those people to independence and a better way of life and a future without American handouts.

America's Global Politics

The political decisions America makes now have global consequences. When the U.S. signs a new trade treaty for importing foreign goods or passes a trade embargo against a nation that ignores human rights, our actions have consequences at home and abroad.

We can welcome a country into "most favored nation" status and greatly enhance its economy -- or we can stop trade with a hostile country and devastate its economic structure. We can take action against a dictatorship by military or nonmilitary means and cause major shifts in that country's government. All the allies of the sanctioned country are affected, too.

Suddenly, their ally has no more means to pay them for weapons or food or medical supplies, and those allied countries suffer also. In a positive sense, American has become the beacon to the world because the decision the U.S. makes regarding any other nation affects the entire globe.

The responsibility is a heavy one that has largely been ignored by Americans. In our day-to-day lives where we have felt safe in the bubble of our own democracy, we have tended to ignore the effects of our actions on other nations. And we often fail to acknowledge The Law of the Consequence: Every action (or non-action) has a consequence.

In 2003, America entered into a military action in Iraq to overthrow the regime of Saddam Hussein because of the potential for biological and possibly nuclear weapons that country could use in terrorist attacks in the U.S. Our fear had been heightened by the September 11, 2001, attack by terrorists on the World Trade Towers and the Pentagon.

The resources America has put into that war have caused consequences not only for the U.S. and Iraq but also for other nations. Countries that traded extensively with Iraq have found a negative impact on their economies as one of their lucrative sources of income was cut off.

The American economy was, in fact, strengthened in some sectors by the war. Iraq found itself without any government and operating under U.S. and United Nations military rule until national elections could be held to start Iraq on the path toward democracy.

Other dictatorships have followed the war closely because they know that they, too, could be the targets of similar military action if they continue human rights violations and pose a threat to the U.S. As the single most powerful nation on the face of the earth, America now controls the safety and welfare of the entire world.

Is There a Runner-Up?

Europeans search for a new democracy. Europe continues to struggle with developing a workable form of democratic government in a short period of time. Despite continued resentment of the U.S., Western European nations want the favorable impacts of democracy on their economies, but so far, they are failing in their efforts.

The European Union's founding members, who have had a loose trading agreement dating back to the 1950s, include France, Germany, Luxembourg, Italy, and the Netherlands, and were later joined by Great Britain.

Today, there are 25 member nations throughout Europe, forming the European Union, or EU, under a treaty established in 1992.

However, to consider the EU to be a United States of Europe would be false. Each country maintains its national identity and internal government, so in some ways it bears a closer resemblance to a loose confederation, much as the United States had under its Articles of Confederation during the years after the American Revolution ended and before a Constitution was adopted in 1789.

The chief flaw of America's Articles of Confederation was a lack of a centralized federal government with any power to enforce the laws it enacted.

Ultimately, the United States found the Articles of Confederation inadequate to allow us to operate as a nation instead of a loose aggregation of separate states, where each state maintained its own interests as paramount. When the European Union's members come to a similar realization, they will have to decide whether to become one nation or merely continue the EU as a trade alliance.

Today the EU remains a federation of separate nations, which in theory, subscribe to common economic, military, health and welfare policies. Each nation has its own national leader and national government, language and customs. The main common ground among EU members has been the adoption of a single currency, the Euro, by 12 of the 25 nations, as well as a common market with a single set of standards for administration and a common policy on agriculture and fisheries.

The EU is a long way from forming a cohesive international governmental policy binding on its members.

Nowhere was this problem of true unity more evident than in the recent failure of the EU nations to adopt a Constitution binding on all members. Instead of following the American Constitution as a model, the EU has attempted unsuccessfully to develop what is essentially an EU-controlled strong central government under which the member nations would be satellite states.

American government is based on the principle of limiting federal powers to those that are essential for the operation of the nation as a whole. All powers not specifically delegated to the U.S. federal government remain with the states.

For example, interstate commerce is regulated federally to facilitate transport of goods and services across the nation.

A federal highway system is regulated by the federal government for the same reason. All fifty states retain the power, among others, to tax goods and services created within their own jurisdictions, to regulate business and the formation of corporations, to enact workers compensation and safety laws, to provide unemployment compensation, and to control professional licensing in medicine and law.

U.S. Congressional action in lawmaking can set minimum standards in many areas, but states can provide more generous benefits than the federal minimum. Thus, the U.S. has a government that is designed to limit central federal power. In contrast, the EU's effort to adopt a constitution has failed because it would establish an international government that could regulate activities which currently do, and should remain, the province of each member nation.

The EU got bogged down in details about vacation time, working hours, and similar details on which each member nation has a vested interest in self-regulation. The proposed constitution was so overreaching that individual nations would have had to cede much of their power to the EU, which they were unwilling to do.

The EU constitutional model is based on a central government that would be so strong that the member states would lack the power to enact legislation which would serve their own citizens' needs.

The EU Constitution sounds more like a Union contract where the government is the employer and the citizens are the employees.

In many ways, the EU model would produce a government that would control the lives of citizens in a way that is just one step removed from some of its former dictatorships.

Why is the EU model and its current failure so important to the U.S.? For one thing, until the EU can agree to act as a union representing all its members, the U.S. will remain the only significant super power in the world. Were all the European nations to join together to form a United States of Europe, eventually they might arrive at super power status as they gained strength and realized common political, economic, and social welfare goals.

But they would have to go far beyond forming a single political entity to become a super power. Currently, the European nations are divided by language, social, customs, tradition and lifestyle.

In contrast, the U.S. has enjoyed a common language and culture for over two centuries. There are no national boundaries separating states in the U.S. Travel from Maine to Hawaii, and the currency will be the same, the economy will be the same, and the American traditions will be the same -- we all celebrate the Fourth of July, Thanksgiving, Memorial Day, and other holidays.

No passports are needed in our travels from state to state, and even allowing for soft Southern accents and Yankee pronunciation, we can all understand each other, we can all do business together, and we can all agree on our personal standards of liberty.

Many U.S. citizens maintain a rich cultural heritage from the lands that they or their ancestors left to journey to America, but no American believes that those traditions can or should supersede our blended American culture.

This type of diversity and harmony is alien to European thinking. They have never experienced the sense of union that exists in America, and they are a long way from even beginning the journey that has taken Americans so far in more than two centuries of national growth.

CHAPTER FIVE
The Journey

Where We Go From Here

By enacting the constitution of the United States our founding fathers put this country on "auto-pilot" and there is no "disengage" switch!!

The only thing we can do as we journey into the future is to control the quality of the "ride" and the "price" we will pay for the voyage! Democracy in its present form may not be a viable concept for the long term but rather one step in political evolution.

In the next few centuries, our current form of government will undoubtedly morph into another more advanced system of government.

The Test of Time

Will our form of democracy survive the test of time? All indications are that it will do so long into the future -- but its fate is, literally, in the hands of the American citizens, who have the power to initiate change in leadership, law, and the direction that America takes on the world stage. Yet it may survive in a form so greatly changed that our definition of democracy will have to change, too.

Our democracy as a representative form of government was termed "The Great Experiment" when our Founding Fathers initiated it with the passage of the U.S. Constitution over two hundred years ago. As we have seen before, the ancient Republic of Rome ended when political conditions changed, and the twenty-first century is a time of massive global political change. What makes us think that America will be any different?

Democracy in its present form is a unique concept. The day will come in the near or distant future when separate national governments will merge into a global political entity.

However, thus far democracy is the best system of government to date which mankind has yet devised, and it would serve us all to remember this.

Democracy is one step in political evolution. But while democracy lasts, we need to protect and preserve the advances it offers over previous forms of government and nurture the liberties it provides.

Our Potential Weakness

American democracy's strength is based on freedom and openness -- but those same traits are also democracy's greatest weaknesses.

A nation that freely shares its information with the public, speaks openly about defense strategies, and invites the rest of the world into the same political arena in a partnership is vulnerable to other nations using the information they gain to their advantage against us.

Our enemies will always try to make Americans pay a bigger and bigger "price" for our way of life. They will try to force us to give up our freedom and openness in favor of security. If we allow that to happen, we will see the freedoms we enjoy disappearing and democracy beginning to slide down a slippery slope toward oblivion.

Until World War II, America had a long-standing tradition of being reluctant to enter any war unless we were attacked first. We felt, and perhaps rightly so before the era of fast transport and global weapons, that our shores were secure.

The attack on Pearl Harbor which triggered our entry into World War II was a watershed event that ended our sense of geographic isolation. Until then, Americans were largely against participating in the war already being waged in Europe, even to defend our allies.

The Price We Pay

Pearl Harbor introduced true global warfare, even in advance of the development of nuclear weapons. We quickly learned that if an enemy can reach America, it can threaten our safety and freedom.

America had to pay a heavy price to maintain democracy during World War II and during the Cold War that ensued. Billions have been spent on shoring up national security, building more powerful weapons, and creating a world-wide intelligence community.

Each time another world power built a more deadly long-range missile, the U.S. countered by building a bigger one, and soon the U.S. built the biggest arsenal of all, at an enormous cost.

We experienced more subtle costs as well. No longer do we say in the words of Emma Lazarus' famous poem at the base of the Statue of Liberty, "Give me your, poor, your tired, your huddled masses, longing to be free..."

By the 1920s, immigration quotas were placed on many countries, and America's borders tightened. Through sad experience, America has lost its trusting attitude toward other nations and the sense of security against an outside attack on our shores, as happened on the infamous date, September 11, 2001.

As the world's only surviving super power, there will always be other nations trying to upset our position to gain more control politically for ideological reasons or in some cases, simply because they resent our power and prosperity and want a bigger piece of the action.

The result so far of tightened security is a high cost in personal freedom. Already airport security measures entail long waiting lines, personal inspections, and generally have reduced the fun in travel except when it's a business necessity.

Homeland Security is costing American taxpayers an extra bite in the federal budget, and this is no longer a short-term emergency response but is becoming a way of life. Soon passports will be required for any travel outside our borders, whereas in the past proof of birth and a photo ID were all that were required to travel to Mexico, the Caribbean, or Canada.

Personal freedom has been one of the hallmarks of American democracy, and it is rapidly changing. As personal freedom continues to erode, our form of democracy is endangered.

We are waging a war in Iraq, where we are seeking to end a rule of tyranny and allow a new emerging democracy a chance to become viable. We are waging a shadow war against terrorists who continue to present a threat to our shores. These wars, and those that will doubtless follow, will increase our costs of democracy substantially.

The price of democracy is getting higher every day, and it will continue to escalate in the future with the current alignment of world powers until it becomes so high that some of us may wonder if it is more than we want to pay. But giving up this system of government would be a price no one wants to pay because at this stage of political evolution, ours is the best system of government ever implemented.

We need to find ways to make democracy continue to work in a troubled world for our own safety and freedom. What will help us do this?

Our Security Blanket

First of all, the U.S. Constitution provides a balanced form of government -- with its powers balanced among three branches, each of which can check the unwarranted use of power by the others.

Previous governments tended to place all power in the hands of a few leaders, or even only one and the rights of citizens could be abused or taken away at will by those in power.

Although no one person or group can seize control of the country under the provisions of the Constitution, we can through fear and inaction allow our rights to be taken away under the guise of protection from foreign threats.

In fact, our choice of elected leaders can determine whether we have officials who seek to preserve freedom and balance it against the needs of national security. The choices we make in our leadership become even more important when American security is threatened by other hostile nations or rogue terrorists.

We Are the "Boatmen"

There is one group that can damage our democracy. They can sabotage it through lethargy, indifference, and a failure to become involved in preserving this Great Experiment for ourselves, our children, and generations yet to come.

That group is "We, the people," as we are called in the Declaration of Independence, and we are a powerful group. We are responsible for electing leaders, for removing inept ones by voting them out of office, and for ensuring that our voices are heard in the House of Representatives, in the Senate chambers, and in the White House.

If we fail to voice our opinions, to let our country's leadership know what we want and do not want, we should have no right to criticize the choices the government makes because we did not make our opinions heard.

If we do not vote, do not get involved in the running of our communities, our states, and our nation, there is always the possibility that our nation will fail to stay on the right track and preserve our democracy.

In short, no one can defeat America but Americans themselves. The only enemy strong enough to destroy our democracy us through an indifference to what is happening in our cities, our nation, and the world.

Participate or
Just Enjoy the "Ride"

This is your call to action, America! To keep our country on the winning track in the future requires you to take an active role now to make that happen.

We live in a time of change, of world crisis, and we must take as much care selecting leaders to watch over our country as we would in selecting someone to care for us or our children.

If we fail to select leaders who can steer our country through a time of crisis, we will get exactly what we deserve -- an unfulfilling democracy. American government was shaped by our Founding Fathers as a participatory government, in which the citizens acted by voting, by taking part in debate, by serving on juries, and by voicing their opinions on political issues.

Yet today, only half the eligible voters in our country go to the ballot box, but the nonvoters are more than ready to voice their dissatisfaction with the election results. For democracy to work, each citizen must take responsibility for making it work.

Be Eternally Vigilant

The Roman Republic worked effectively as long as its citizens promoted the common good of their country above personal gain. Only when greed and corruption crept in -- and when citizens of the Republic put their own welfare above that of their nation -- did the Republic started to fail. Each person was expected to cooperate with everyone else to reap the rewards that they all worked for together. They believed that there were three main elements to effective government:

- Civic virtue
- Moral education, and
- Participation in civic affairs at the community level.

Of all these, they believed that civic virtue -- the most important of their values -- was demonstrated when they set aside their own personal desires for the good of the community.

The people had far fewer rights than we do today because they were expected to be a part of the whole, working for a common end. The United States is hardly a form of Classical Republicanism. However, we can learn from this form and incorporate some of its ideology to improve our government.

Like the leaders of the Roman Republic, our Founding Fathers built a Constitution founded on the belief that civic virtue is a matter of action, not merely right thinking. It is not enough to believe in freedom and participatory government -- each of us must act by taking part in improving our communities, our state, and our nation. Our democracy will survive, but the "burden" of maintaining its survival rests with us.

When we ignore what is taking place in the national and international political arenas in favor of focusing solely on ourselves, democracy begins to erode. When we stay away from election polls, it erodes a bit more. When we fail to educate ourselves by reading in depth about what is happening in our government and around the world and acting on that knowledge, democracy begins to decay.

We must, as citizens, be constantly vigilant if democracy is to survive in its current form. When our leaders meet our needs and act in the way that best serves our nation, we can act by re-electing them. If we have corrupt leaders, we can act by voting them out of office and ensuring that they are censured in the courts.

Thomas Paine said that "the price of liberty is eternal vigilance." To secure our liberty for the years ahead, to ensure that democracy remains viable as a form of government, we must take the responsibility for its welfare. To do otherwise is to ensure that democracy will fail.

CHAPTER SIX
Information or Conformation

Think America. Think!

Think as a matter of habit. Intellectually we all know that there is no substitute for thinking. However most of the time we fail to observe, analyze, and reason because we believe there are others more knowledgeable on a particular subject.

Naturally it is more comforting to align ourselves with those whom we know, respect, and trust. However, we have to keep in mind that providing information to the public is a profession or a duty. People do it for a living or as part of their job. Consequently, they must and will present issues consistent with their former position and also try to comply with expectation based on their status and position in the society.

People in the media must present news in a marketable package for public consumption.

To a certain extent we all have a hidden agenda when we speak!! We speak what we believe is the truth and have the tendency to "stack the deck" in order to support our position on an issue.

Think For Yourself

Many of us only pay attention to issues in the country that affect us personally -- when taxes go up, when a law is passed that we don't like, or when we find that a loved one is going off to war. Yet it is important to understand the issues affecting America on a global scale -- and to pay attention to what is happening and understand the causes of crises throughout the world.

The individual who keeps his brain in neutral is likely to find that others are manipulating him – shifting his mental gears for him. And many people tend to reduce complex, interdependent world problems to simple issues, ignoring the other problems that are causally related to the current crisis.

Our Values in Communication

We have to keep in mind that telling the truth and being fair, honest and sincere are human traits and are applicable only in a one-on-one, person-to-person line of communication.

In politics things are more complex than they appear, and those personal values do not apply.

Countries and international institutions as a whole are entities. The person speaking on behalf of an entity or about an event will always express whatever is in the best interest of the people who are part of that entity at a given time and place. Therefore, issues regarding rights and wrongs need to be viewed with open mind because they are perceived differently by the citizens of different nations.

The beliefs of the people of any nation correspond to their history, cultural or religious background. Consequently, it is possible for two people to make statements that are diametrically different concerning the same issue, and both can be right or wrong in the same time.

Information Galore

We are inundated with information twenty-four hours a day in a form of sound bites, video clips, and rumors. To separate news from "noise" is getting more difficult by the day. All of what we see and hear influences our mood, our spirit, and our general well-being, depending on the way we relate to the issue at hand.

Today, television is the major news source for American households. It is also a major force in shaping public opinion. We would like to believe that the newscasts provide factual, unbiased reporting of world and national events and crises. The truth is that the networks need to be profitable operations.

For the sake of their economic survival, they must provide what the people are interested in hearing, and that determines the content, slant, and type of news which gets reported.

Consequently, the networks and the media in general are not, as many people may believe, informing the public about events so much as trying to capture viewers. The greater the viewership, the more ads the network can sell, and the more ads the network sells, the more profitable it will be, and the more profitable the network is, the happier the share-holders are.

The national networks provide the news in sound bites and video bites, giving "headlines" rather than presenting neutral views. Even when the facts stated are correct, they are slanted and oversimplified in order to make the news coverage sell.

The same standards of analytical thinking need to be applied to what you see and hear on the news as they do to information you receive from any other authority.

Our Hidden Agenda

We are living in a free society and are free to speak our minds. We all have a hidden agenda which is that we believe we are right and want to convince others about our point of view.

So when we speak, it is natural for us to present our case as fact or truth, as we see it or believe it or know it. The reasons we give for stating our opinions as fact are many: I saw it myself, I heard it with my own ears, or I heard it from someone I trust.

Keep in mind that the people we see delivering the news or plugging a product or a promise on television, who are presented as experts, also "believe" they are right. They are hailed by others as authorities in their fields, so they should be a reputable source of information. After all, why shouldn't you trust someone who is an authority on the subject matter, right?

They have all the facts and can spew statistics to back up their position on an issue. They have done the research, so their statements can be trusted.

Beware! What their presenting may just be what they "believe" to be right, appropriate, or correct, and you should wonder if that is what you can identify for yourself as true. It is too easy to accept someone's rhetoric and biased opinions as fact.

Things that sound right must *be* right, you might say. How many times have you heard a supposed authority on world problems making statements like these: "If we can put a man on the moon, we should be able to end world hunger" ... or "cure cancer" ... or "end poverty"?

Take your pick. There's always a crisis for which an expert has a simple solution, or at least a solution that sounds simple from the way he presents it.

The Voice of Authority

When we were children, we looked up to the adults around us. They appeared to be authorities on just about everything -- as children, we believed they had all the answers.

Our parents, teachers, ministers, scout leaders, and other adults seemed to understand how the world worked and answered our questions. We accepted what they said as true.

As adults, we have learned that many of the explanations we received as children were oversimplified, edited to fit a child's ability to comprehend, or in some cases, we were told falsehoods because adults believed that we couldn't understand the truth.

Here's a tip: Today many authorities treat their listeners as if they were children.

Recognizing the voice of authority isn't always easy because authorities come disguised in many forms. Learning to spot false claims and those that have enough truth in the content to seem credible can be tricky.

When you accept the views of experts without determining for yourself what is true, you are adopting that authority's ideas as your own. It's an easy way out. It doesn't require checking the facts you hear, researching the issues involved, and then arriving at a reasoned opinion yourself. It's much easier to accept what authorities say because they are, after all, experts who should have in-depth information on their subject area.

Perhaps they do, but many authorities and experts offer simple solutions to complex problems, lulling their listeners into the false belief that there are easy answers to everything.

Put Your Brain in Gear

It is time to *wake up*, America! We're adults now and need to put aside childish, unquestioning reliance on authorities for our opinions and believe whatever we're told, whether it's a statement by a politician about the reasons for fighting a war, the causes of poverty, or a rationale that taxes must be raised to keep Social Security solvent.

All the pronouncements made to us by authorities, experts, politicians, and pollsters may or may not be accurate.

The only way to know for sure is to put our own brains in gear, and sort out for ourselves whether what we are being told is fact or opinion, or in some cases, an outright lie.

Analyzing the information you receive is not always a quick and easy task, making it simpler to rely on the experts for information. It takes research, study, and effort to review not only what an authority says but also whether what he says is accurate. You need to invest your time, energy, and thought in arriving at your own decision.

Only after analyzing critically what you are told can you determine the truth of what experts say. Then you can you make informed decisions when you select your next Congressional Representative or your next physician or your next employer. Making a mistake can be very costly for you personally and ultimately, for our country.

Putting your brain in gear may be painful at first because it requires you to think before forming an opinion, to search out facts for yourself, and only then to form an opinion of your own. The next time someone tells you what America's position is, or should be, on peacekeeping efforts throughout the world, on outsourcing jobs to third-world countries, or on the financial crisis in Social Security, ask where they got their facts.

In this new communication revolution we are communicating across the globe and across historical and cultural boundaries. Unless we qualify what we hear and what we say, we can confuse ourselves as well as others and may make us do things that we or our children will regret now and in the future.

Over 2500 years ago, Prince Gautama Siddhartha, who became known as the Buddha, advised his followers to think:

- *Do not believe in anything simply because you have heard it.*
- *Do not believe in anything simply because it is found written.*
- *Do not believe in anything simply because it is spoken and rumored by many.*
- *But after observation and analysis, when you find that anything agrees with reason and is conducive to the good and benefit of one and all, then accept it and live up to it.*

That advice was good then and is still good today. To examine issues critically, to come to your own conclusions, and to think for yourself is your right as an American.

Don't let anyone else take this right away from you by blindly letting a "respected or perceived" authority tell you what to think!

EXHIBITS

THE DECLARATION OF INDEPENDENCE

A transcript.

The text is formatted to enhance readability.
Capitalization and spelling of words kept in its original form.

IN CONGRESS
July 4, 1776

THE UNANIMOUS DECLARATION OF THE THIRTEEN UNITED STATES OF AMERICA,

When in the Course of human events, it becomes necessary for one people to dissolve the political bands which have connected them with another, and to assume among the powers of the earth, the separate and equal station to which the Laws of Nature and of Nature's God entitle them, a decent respect to the opinions of mankind requires that they should declare the causes which impel them to the separation.

We hold these truths to be self-evident, that all men are created equal, that they are endowed by their Creator with certain unalienable Rights, that among these are Life, Liberty and the pursuit of Happiness.-- That to secure these rights, Governments are instituted among Men, deriving their just powers from the consent of the governed, --That whenever any form of

Government becomes destructive of these ends, it is the Right of the People to alter or to abolish it, and to institute new Government, laying its foundation on such principles and organizing its powers in such form, as to them shall seem most likely to effect their Safety and Happiness. Prudence, indeed, will dictate that Governments long established should not be changed for light and transient causes; and accordingly all experience hath shown, that mankind are more disposed to suffer, while evils are sufferable, than to right themselves by abolishing the forms to which they are accustomed.

But when a long train of abuses and usurpations, pursuing invariably the same Object evinces a design to reduce them under absolute Despotism, it is their right, it is their duty, to throw off such Government, and to provide new Guards for their future security.--Such has been the patient sufferance of these Colonies; and such is now the necessity which constrains them to alter their former Systems of Government.

The history of the present King of Great Britain is a history of repeated injuries and usurpations, all having in direct object the establishment of an absolute Tyranny over these States. To prove this, let Facts be submitted to a candid world.

He has refused his Assent to Laws, the most wholesome and necessary for the public good.

He has forbidden his Governors to pass Laws of immediate and pressing importance, unless suspended in their operation till his Assent should be obtained; and when so suspended, he has utterly neglected to attend to them.

He has refused to pass other Laws for the accommodation of large districts of people, unless those people would relinquish the right of Representation in the Legislature, a right inestimable to them and formidable to tyrants only.

He has called together legislative bodies at places unusual, uncomfortable, and distant from the depository of their public Records, for the sole purpose of fatiguing them into compliance with his measures.

He has dissolved Representative Houses repeatedly, for opposing with manly firmness his invasions on the rights of the people.

He has refused for a long time, after such dissolutions, to cause others to be elected; whereby the Legislative powers, incapable of Annihilation, have returned to the People at large for their exercise; the State remaining in the mean time exposed to all the dangers of invasion from without, and convulsions within.

He has endeavored to prevent the population of these States; for that purpose obstructing the Laws for Naturalization of Foreigners; refusing to pass others to encourage their migrations hither, and raising the conditions of new Appropriations of Lands.

He has obstructed the Administration of Justice, by refusing his Assent to Laws for establishing Judiciary powers.

He has made Judges dependent on his Will alone, for the tenure of their offices, and the amount and payment of their salaries.

He has erected a multitude of New Offices, and sent hither swarms of Officers to harass our people, and eat out their substance.

He has kept among us, in times of peace, Standing Armies without the Consent of our legislatures.

He has affected to render the Military independent of and superior to the Civil power.

He has combined with others to subject us to a jurisdiction foreign to our constitution, and unacknowledged by our laws; giving his Assent to their Acts of pretended Legislation: For Quartering large bodies of armed troops among us: For protecting them, by a mock Trial, from punishment for any Murders which they should commit on the Inhabitants of these States:

> For cutting off our Trade with all parts of the world:

➢ For imposing Taxes on us without our Consent:

➢ For depriving us in many cases, of the benefits of Trial by jury:

➢ For transporting us beyond Seas to be tried for pretended Offences

➢ For abolishing the free System of English Laws in a neighboring Province, establishing therein an Arbitrary government, and enlarging its Boundaries so as to render it at once an example and fit instrument for introducing the same absolute rule into these Colonies:

➢ For taking away our Charters, abolishing our most valuable Laws, and altering fundamentally the Forms of our Governments:

➢ For suspending our own Legislatures, and declaring themselves invested with power to legislate for us in all cases whatsoever.

➢ He has abdicated Government here, by declaring us out of his Protection and waging War against us.

➢ He has plundered our seas, ravaged our Coasts, burnt our towns, and destroyed the lives of our people.

➢ He is at this time transporting large Armies of foreign Mercenaries to complete the works of death, desolation and tyranny, already begun with circumstances of Cruelty & perfidy scarcely paralleled in the most barbarous ages, and totally unworthy the Head of a civilized nation.

➢ He has constrained our fellow Citizens taken Captive on the high Seas to bear Arms against their Country, to become the executioners of their friends and Brethren, or to fall themselves by their Hands.

➢ He has excited domestic insurrections amongst us, and has endeavored to bring on the inhabitants of our frontiers, the merciless Indian Savages, whose known rule of warfare is an undistinguished destruction of all ages, sexes and conditions.

In every stage of these Oppressions We have petitioned for Redress in the most humble terms: Our repeated Petitions have been answered only by repeated injury. A Prince, whose character is thus marked by every act which may define a Tyrant, is unfit to be the ruler of a free people.

Nor have we been wanting in attentions to our British brethren. We have warned them from time to time of attempts by their legislature to extend an unwarrantable jurisdiction over us. We have reminded them of the circumstances of our emigration and settlement here.

We have appealed to their native justice and magnanimity, and we have conjured them by the ties of our common kindred to disavow these usurpations, which would inevitably interrupt our connections and correspondence.

They too have been deaf to the voice of justice and of consanguinity. We must, therefore, acquiesce in the necessity, which denounces our Separation, and hold them, as we hold the rest of mankind, Enemies in War, in Peace Friends.

We, therefore, the Representatives of the united States of America, in General Congress, Assembled, appealing to the Supreme Judge of the world for the rectitude of our intentions, do, in the Name, and by Authority of the good People of these Colonies, solemnly publish and declare, That these United Colonies are, and of Right ought to be Free and Independent States; that they are Absolved from all Allegiance to the British Crown, and that all political connection between them and the State of Great Britain, is and ought to be totally dissolved; and that as Free and Independent States, they have full Power to levy War, conclude Peace, contract Alliances, establish Commerce, and to do all other Acts and Things which Independent States may of right do.

And for the support of this Declaration, with a firm reliance on the protection of divine Providence, we mutually pledge to each other our Lives, our Fortunes and our sacred Honor.

Note: The 56 signatures on the Declaration appear in the positions indicated:

COLUMN ONE
GEORGIA

Button Gwinnett
Lyman Hall
George Walton

COLUMN TWO
NORTH CAROLINA

William Hooper
Joseph Hewes
John Penn

SOUTH CAROLINA

Edward Rutledge
Thomas Heyward, Jr.
Thomas Lynch, Jr.
Arthur Middleton

COLUMN THREE
MASSACHUSETTS

John Hancock

MARYLAND

Samuel Chase
William Paca
Thomas Stone
Charles Carroll of Carrollton

VIRGINIA

George Wythe
Richard Henry Lee
Thomas Jefferson
Benjamin Harrison
Thomas Nelson, Jr.

Francis Lightfoot Lee
Carter Braxton

COLUMN FOUR

PENNSYLVANIA

Robert Morris
Benjamin Rush
Benjamin Franklin
John Morton
George Clymer
James Smith
George Taylor
James Wilson
George Ross

DELAWARE

Caesar Rodney
George Read
Thomas McKean

COLUMN FIVE

NEW YORK

William Floyd
Philip Livingston
Francis Lewis
Lewis Morris

NEW JERSEY

Richard Stockton
John Witherspoon
Francis Hopkinson

John Hart
Abraham Clark

COLUMN SIX

NEW HAMPSHIRE

Josiah Bartlett
William Whipple

MASSACHUSETTS

Samuel Adams
John Adams

Robert Treat Paine
Elbridge Gerry

RHODE ISLAND

Stephen Hopkins
William Ellery

CONNECTICUT

Roger Sherman
Samuel Huntington
William Williams
Oliver Wolcott

NEW HAMPSHIRE

Matthew Thornton

THE ARTICLES OF CONFEDERATION

Agreed to by Congress November 15, 1777;
Ratified and in force, March 1, 1781.

PREAMBLE. To all to whom these Presents shall come, we the undersigned Delegates of the States affixed to our Names end greeting.

Articles of Confederation and perpetual Union between the States of New Hampshire, Massachusetts bay, Rhode Island and Providence Plantations, Connecticut, New York, New Jersey, Pennsylvania, Delaware, Maryland, Virginia, North Carolina, South Carolina and Georgia

ARTICLE I.

The Stile of this Confederacy shall be "The United States of America."

ARTICLE II.

Each state retains its sovereignty, freedom, and independence, and every power, jurisdiction, and right, which is not by this Confederation expressly delegated to the United States, in Congress assembled.

ARTICLE III.

The said States hereby severally enter into a firm league of friendship with each other, for their common defense, the security of their liberties, and their mutual and general welfare, binding themselves to assist each other, against all force offered to, or attacks made upon them, or any of them, on account of religion, sovereignty, trade, or any other pretense whatever.

ARTICLE IV.

The better to secure and perpetuate mutual friendship and intercourse among the people of the different States in this Union, the free inhabitants of each of these States, paupers, vagabonds, and fugitives from justice excepted, shall be entitled to all privileges and immunities of free citizens in the several States; and the people of each State shall free ingress and regress to and from any other State, and shall enjoy therein all the privileges of trade and commerce, subject to the same duties, impositions, and restrictions as the inhabitants thereof respectively, provided that such restrictions shall not extend so far as to prevent the removal of property imported into any State, to any other State, of which the owner is an inhabitant; provided also that no imposition, duties or restriction shall be laid by any State, on the property of the United States, or either of them.

If any person guilty of, or charged with, treason, felony, or other high misdemeanor in any State, shall flee from justice, and be found in any of the United States, he shall, upon demand of the Governor or executive power of the State from which he fled, be delivered up and removed to the State having jurisdiction of his offense.

Full faith and credit shall be given in each of these States to the records, acts, and judicial proceedings of the courts and magistrates of every other State.

ARTICLE V.

For the most convenient management of the general interests of the United States, delegates shall be annually appointed in such manner as the legislatures of each State shall direct, to meet in Congress on the first Monday in November, in every year, with a power reserved to each State to recall its delegates, or any of them, at any time within the year, and to send others in their stead for the remainder of the year.

No State shall be represented in Congress by less than two, nor more than seven members; and no person shall be capable of being a delegate for more than three years in any term of six years; nor shall any person, being a delegate, be capable of holding any office under the United States, for which he, or another for his benefit, receives any salary, fees or emolument of any kind.

Each State shall maintain its own delegates in a meeting of the States, and while they act as members of the committee of the States.

In determining questions in the United States in Congress assembled, each State shall have one vote.

Freedom of speech and debate in Congress shall not be impeached or questioned in any court or place out of Congress, and the members of Congress shall be protected in their persons from arrests or imprisonments, during the time of their going to and from, and attendance on Congress, except for treason, felony, or breach of the peace.

ARTICLE VI.

No State, without the consent of the United States in Congress assembled, shall send any embassy to, or receive any embassy from, or enter into any conference, agreement, alliance or treaty with any King, Prince or State; nor shall any person holding any office of profit or trust under the United States, or any of them, accept any present, emolument, office or title of any kind whatever from any King, Prince or foreign State; nor shall the United States in Congress assembled, or any of them, grant any title of nobility.

No two or more States shall enter into any treaty, confederation or alliance whatever between them, without the consent of the United States in Congress assembled, specifying accurately the purposes for which the same is to be entered into, and how long it shall continue.

No State shall lay any imposts or duties, which may interfere with any stipulations in treaties, entered into by the United States in Congress assembled, with any King, Prince or State, in pursuance of any treaties already proposed by Congress, to the courts of France and Spain.

No vessel of war shall be kept up in time of peace by any State, except such number only, as shall be deemed necessary by the United States in Congress assembled, for the defense of such State, or its trade; nor shall any body of forces be kept up by any State in time of peace, except such number only, as in the judgment of the United States in Congress assembled, shall be deemed requisite to garrison the forts necessary for the defense of such State; but every State shall always keep up a well-regulated and disciplined militia, sufficiently armed and accoutered, and shall provide and constantly have ready for use, in public stores, a due number of filed pieces and tents, and a proper quantity of arms, ammunition and camp equipage.

No State shall engage in any war without the consent of the United States in Congress assembled, unless such State be actually invaded by enemies, or shall have received certain advice of a resolution being formed by some nation of Indians to invade such State, and the danger is so imminent as not to admit of a delay till the United States in Congress assembled can be consulted; nor shall any State grant commissions to any ships or vessels of war, nor letters of marque or reprisal, except it be after a declaration of war by the United States in Congress assembled, and then only against the Kingdom or State and the subjects thereof, against which war has been so declared, and under such regulations as shall be established by the United States in Congress assembled, unless such State be infested by pirates, in which case vessels of war may be fitted out for that occasion, and kept so long as the danger shall continue, or until the United States in Congress assembled shall determine otherwise.

ARTICLE VII.

When land forces are raised by any State for the common defense, all officers of or under the rank of colonel, shall be appointed by the legislature of each State respectively, by whom such forces shall be raised, or in such manner as such State shall direct, and all vacancies shall be filled up by the State which first made the appointment.

ARTICLE VIII.

All charges of war, and all other expenses that shall be incurred for the common defense or general welfare, and allowed by the United States in Congress assembled, shall be defrayed out of a common treasury, which shall be supplied by the several States in proportion to the value of all land within each State, granted or surveyed for any

person, as such land and the buildings and improvements thereon shall be estimated according to such mode as the United States in Congress assembled, shall from time to time direct and appoint.

The taxes for paying that proportion shall be laid and levied by the authority and direction of the legislatures of the several States within the time agreed upon by the United States in Congress assembled.

ARTICLE IX.

The United States in Congress assembled, shall have the sole and exclusive right and power of determining on peace and war, except in the cases mentioned in the sixth article -- of sending and receiving ambassadors -- entering into treaties and alliances, provided that no treaty of commerce shall be made whereby the legislative power of the respective States shall be restrained from imposing such imposts and duties on foreigners, as their own people are subjected to, or from prohibiting the exportation or importation of any species of goods or commodities whatsoever -- of establishing rules for deciding in all cases, what captures on land or water shall be legal, and in what manner prizes taken by land or naval forces in the service of the United States shall be divided or appropriated -- of granting

letters of marquee and reprisal in times of peace --
appointing courts for the trial of piracies and felonies
committed on the high seas and establishing
courts for receiving and determining finally appeals
in all cases of captures, provided that no member of
Congress shall be appointed a judge of any of the said
courts.

The United States in Congress assembled shall
also be the last resort on appeal in all disputes and
differences now subsisting or that hereafter may arise
between two or more States concerning boundary,
jurisdiction or any other causes whatever; which
authority shall always be exercised in the manner
following. Whenever the legislative or executive
authority or lawful agent of any State in controversy
with another shall present a petition to Congress
stating the matter in question and praying for a
hearing, notice thereof shall be given by order of
Congress to the legislative or executive authority of
the other State in controversy, and a day assigned for
the appearance of the parties by their lawful agents,
who shall then be directed to appoint by joint
consent, commissioners or judges to constitute a
court for hearing and determining the matter in
question: but if they cannot agree, Congress shall
name three persons out of each of the United States,
and from the list of such persons each party shall
alternately strike out one, the petitioners beginning,
until the number shall be reduced to thirteen; and
from that number not less than seven, nor more

than nine names as Congress shall direct, shall in the presence of Congress be drawn out by lot, and the persons whose names shall be so drawn or any five of them, shall be commissioners or judges, to

hear and finally determine the controversy, so always as a major part of the judges who shall hear the cause shall agree in the determination: and if either party shall neglect to attend at the day appointed, without showing reasons, which Congress shall judge sufficient, or being present shall refuse to strike, the Congress shall proceed to nominate three persons out of each State, and the secretary of Congress shall strike in behalf of such party absent or refusing; and the judgment and sentence of the court to be appointed, in the manner before prescribed, shall be final and conclusive; and if any of the parties shall refuse to submit to the authority of such court, or to appear or defend their claim or cause, the court shall nevertheless proceed to pronounce sentence, or judgment, which shall in like manner be final and decisive, the judgment or sentence and other proceedings being in either case transmitted to Congress, and lodged among the acts of Congress for the security of the parties concerned: provided that every commissioner, before he sits in judgment, shall take an oath to be administered by one of the judges of the supreme or superior court of the State, where the cause shall be tried, 'well and truly to hear and determine the matter in question, according to the best of his judgment, without favor, affection or hope of reward': provided also, that no State shall be deprived of territory for the benefit of the United States. All controversies concerning the private right of soil claimed under different grants of two or more States, whose jurisdictions as they may respect such lands, and the States which passed such grants are adjusted, the said grants or either of them being at the same time claimed to have originated antecedent to such settlement of jurisdiction, shall on the petition of either party to the Congress of the United States, be finally determined as near as may be in the same manner as is before prescribed for deciding disputes respecting territorial jurisdiction between different States.

The United States in Congress assembled shall also have the sole and exclusive right and power of regulating the alloy and value of coin struck by their own authority, or by that of the respective States -- fixing the standards of weights and measures throughout the United States -- regulating the trade and managing all affairs with the Indians, not members of any of the States, provided that the legislative right of any State within its own limits be not infringed or violated -- establishing or regulating post offices from one State to another, throughout all the United States, and exacting such postage on the papers passing through the same as may be requisite to defray the expenses of the said office -- appointing all officers of the land forces, in the service of the United States, excepting regimental officers -- appointing all the officers of the naval forces, and commissioning all officers whatever in the service of the United States -- making rules for the government and regulation of the said land and naval forces, and directing their operations.

The United States in Congress assembled shall have authority to appoint a committee, to sit in the

recess of Congress, to be denominated 'A Committee of the States', and to consist of one delegate from each State; and to appoint such other committees and civil officers as may be necessary for managing the general affairs of the United States under their direction -- to appoint one of their members to preside, provided that no person be allowed to serve in the office of president more than one year in any term of three years; to ascertain the necessary sums of money to be raised for the service of the United States, and to appropriate and apply the same for defraying the public expenses -- to borrow money, or emit bills on the credit of the United States, transmitting every half-year to the respective States an account of the sums of money so borrowed or emitted -- to build and equip a navy -- to agree upon the number of land forces, and to make requisitions from each State for its quota, in proportion to the number of white inhabitants in such State; which requisition shall be binding, and thereupon the legislature of each State shall appoint the regimental officers, raise the men and clothe, arm and equip them in a solid- like manner, at the expense of the

United States; and the officers and men so clothed, armed and equipped shall march to the place appointed, and within the time agreed on by the United States in Congress assembled.

But if the United States in Congress assembled shall, on consideration of circumstances judge proper that any State should not raise men, or should raise a smaller number of men than the quota thereof, such extra number shall be raised,

officered, clothed, armed and equipped in the same manner as the quota of each State, unless the legislature of such State shall judge that such extra number cannot be safely spread out in the same, in which case they shall raise, officer, clothe, arm and equip as many of such extra number as they judge can be safely spared. And the officers and men so clothed, armed, and equipped, shall march to the place appointed, and within the time agreed on by the United States in Congress assembled.

The United States in Congress assembled shall never engage in a war, nor grant letters of marquee or reprisal in time of peace, nor enter into any treaties or alliances, nor coin money, nor regulate the value thereof, nor ascertain the sums and expenses necessary for the defense and welfare of the United States, or any of them, nor emit bills, nor borrow money on the credit of the United States, nor appropriate money, nor agree upon the number of vessels of war, to be built or purchased, or the number of land or sea forces to be raised, nor appoint a commander in chief of the army or navy, unless nine States assent to the same: nor shall a question on any other point, except for adjourning from day to day be determined, unless by the votes of the majority of the United States in Congress assembled.

The Congress of the United States shall have power to adjourn to any time within the year, and to any place within the United States, so that no period of adjournment be for a longer duration than the space of six months, and shall publish the journal of their proceedings monthly, except such parts thereof relating to treaties, alliances or military operations, as in their judgment require secrecy; and the yeas and nays of the delegates of each State on any question shall be entered on the journal, when it is desired by any delegates of a State, or any of them, at his or their request shall be furnished with a transcript of the said journal, except such parts as are above excepted, to lay before the legislatures of the several States.

ARTICLE X.

The Committee of the States, or any nine of them, shall be authorized to execute, in the recess of Congress, such of the powers of Congress as the United States in Congress assembled, by the consent of the nine States, shall from time to time think expedient to vest them with; provided that no power be delegated to the said Committee, for the exercise

of which, by the Articles of Confederation, the voice of nine States in the Congress of the United States assembled be requisite.

ARTICLE XI.

Canada acceding to this confederation, and adjoining in the measures of the United States, shall be admitted into, and entitled to all the advantages of this Union; but no other colony shall be admitted into the same, unless such admission be agreed to by nine States.

ARTICLE XII.

All bills of credit emitted, monies borrowed, and debts contracted by, or under the authority of Congress, before the assembling of the United States, in pursuance of the present confederation, shall be deemed and considered as a charge against the United States, for payment and satisfaction whereof the said United States, and the public faith are hereby solemnly pledged.

ARTICLE XIII.

Every State shall abide by the determination of the United States in Congress assembled, on all questions which by this confederation are submitted to them. And the Articles of this Confederation shall be inviolably observed by every State, and the Union shall be perpetual; nor shall any alteration at any time hereafter be made in any of them; unless such alteration be agreed to in a Congress of the United States, and be afterwards confirmed by the legislatures of every State. And whereas it hath pleased the Great Governor of the World to incline the hearts of the legislatures we respectively represent in Congress, to approve of, and to authorize us to ratify the said Articles of Confederation and perpetual Union. Know Ye that we the undersigned delegates, by virtue of the power and authority to us given for that purpose, do by these presents, in the name and in behalf of our respective constituents, fully and entirely ratify and confirm each and every of the said Articles of Confederation and perpetual Union, and all and singular the matters and things therein contained: And we do further solemnly plight and engage the faith of our respective constituents, that they shall abide by the determinations of the United States in Congress assembled, on all questions, which by the said Confederation are submitted to them. And that the Articles thereof shall be inviolably observed by the

States we respectively represent, and that the Union shall be perpetual.

In witness whereof we have hereunto set our hands in Congress. Done at Philadelphia in the State of Pennsylvania on the Ninth day of July in the Year of our Lord One Thousand Seven Hundred and Seventy-Eight, and in the Third Year of the independence of America.

On the part and behalf of the State of
NEW HAMPSHIRE

Josiah Bartlett
John Wentworth Junior. August 8th 1778

On the part and behalf of The State of
MASSACHUSETTS BAY

John Hancock
Samuel Adams
Elbridge Gerry
Francis Dana
James Lovell
Samuel Holten

On the part and behalf of the State of
RHODE ISLAND AND
PROVIDENCE PLANTATIONS:

William Ellery
Henry Marchant
John Collins

On the part and behalf of the State of
CONNECTICUT

Roger Sherman
Samuel Huntington
Oliver Wolcott
Titus Hosmer
Andrew Adams

On the Part and Behalf of the State of
NEW YORK

James   *Duane*
Francis   *Lewis*
Wm   *Duer*
Gouv Morris

On the Part and in Behalf of the State of
NEW JERSEY
November 26, 1778

Jno Witherspoon
Nath. Scudder

On the part and behalf of the State of
PENNSYLVANIA

Robt Morris
Daniel Roberdeau
John Bayard Smith
William Clingan
Joseph Reed July 22, 1778

On the part and behalf of the State of
DELAWARE

Tho Mckean, February 12, 1779

John Dickinson, May 5th 1779

Nicholas Van Dyke

On the part and behalf of the State of
MARYLAND:

John Hanson, March 1 1781
Daniel Carroll

On the Part and Behalf of the State of
VIRGINIA

Richard Henry Lee

John Banister

Thomas Adams

Jno Harvie

Francis Lightfoot Lee

On the part and Behalf of the State of
NORTH CAROLINA

John Penn, July 21st 1778

Corns Harnett

Jno Williams

On the part and behalf of the State of
SOUTH CAROLINA

Henry Laurens
William Henry Drayton
Jno Mathews
Richd Hutson
Thos Heyward Junr

On the part and behalf of the State of
GEORGIA

Jno Walton, July 24, 1778

Edwd Telfair

Edwd Langworthy

THE CONSTITUTION
OF THE
UNITED STATES OF AMERICA

A Transcription

Note: The following text is a transcription of the Constitution from its original form. Text underlined have since amended or superseded.

We the People of the United States, in Order to form a more perfect Union, establish Justice, insure domestic Tranquility, provide for the common defense, promote the general Welfare, and secure the Blessings of Liberty to ourselves and our Posterity, do ordain and establish this Constitution for the United States of America.

ARTICLE I.

SECTION 1. All legislative Powers herein granted shall be vested in a Congress of the United States, which shall consist of a Senate and House of Representatives.

SECTION 2. The House of Representatives shall be composed of Members chosen every second Year by the People of the several States, and the Electors in each State shall have the Qualifications requisite for Electors of the most numerous Branch of the State Legislature.

No Person shall be a Representative who shall not have attained to the Age of twenty five Years, and been seven Years a Citizen of the United States, and who shall not, when elected, be an Inhabitant of that State in which he shall be chosen.

<u>Representatives and direct Taxes shall be apportioned among the several States which may be included within this Union, according to their respective Numbers, which shall be determined by adding to the whole Number of free Persons, including those bound to Service for a Term of Years, and excluding Indians not taxed, three fifths of all other Persons</u>. The actual Enumeration shall be made within three Years after the first Meeting of the Congress of the United States, and within every subsequent Term of ten Years, in such Manner as they shall by Law direct. The Number of Representatives shall not exceed one for every thirty Thousand, but each State shall have at Least one Representative; and until such enumeration shall be made, the State of New Hampshire shall be entitled to chuse three, Massachusetts eight, Rhode-Island and Providence Plantations one, Connecticut five, New-York six, New Jersey four, Pennsylvania eight, Delaware one, Maryland six, Virginia ten, North Carolina five, South Carolina five, and Georgia three.

When vacancies happen in the Representation from any State, the Executive Authority thereof shall issue Writs of Election to fill such Vacancies.

The House of Representatives shall chuse their Speaker and other Officers; and shall have the sole Power of Impeachment.

SECTION 3. The Senate of the United States shall be composed of two Senators from each State, chosen by the Legislature thereof for six Years; and each Senator shall have one Vote.

Immediately after they shall be assembled in Consequence of the first Election, they shall be divided as equally as may be into three Classes. The Seats of the Senators of the first Class shall be vacated at the Expiration of the second Year, of the second Class at the Expiration of the fourth Year, and of the third Class at the Expiration of the sixth Year, so that one third may be chosen every second Year; and if Vacancies happen by Resignation, or otherwise, during the Recess of the Legislature of any State, the Executive thereof may make temporary Appointments until the next Meeting of the Legislature, which shall then fill such Vacancies.

No Person shall be a Senator who shall not have attained to the Age of thirty Years, and been nine Years a Citizen of the United States, and who shall not, when elected, be an Inhabitant of that State for which he shall be chosen.

The Vice President of the United States shall be President of the Senate, but shall have no Vote, unless they be equally divided.

The Senate shall chuse their other Officers, and also a President pro tempore, in the Absence of the Vice President, or when he shall exercise the Office of President of the United States.

The Senate shall have the sole Power to try all Impeachments. When sitting for that Purpose, they shall be on Oath or Affirmation. When the President of the United States is tried, the Chief Justice shall preside: And no Person shall be convicted without the Concurrence of two thirds of the Members present.

Judgment in Cases of Impeachment shall not extend further than to removal from Office, and disqualification to hold and enjoy any Office of honor, Trust or Profit under the United States: but the Party convicted shall nevertheless be liable and subject to Indictment, Trial, Judgment and Punishment, according to Law.

SECTION 4. The Times, Places and Manner of holding Elections for Senators and Representatives, shall be prescribed in each State by the Legislature thereof; but the Congress may at any time by Law make or alter such Regulations, except as to the Places of choosing Senators.

The Congress shall assemble at least once in every Year, and such Meeting shall be on the first

Monday in December, unless they shall by Law appoint a different Day.

SECTION 5. Each House shall be the Judge of the Elections, Returns and Qualifications of its own Members, and a Majority of each shall constitute a Quorum to do Business; but a smaller Number may adjourn from day to day, and may be authorized to compel the Attendance of absent Members, in such Manner, and under such Penalties as each House may provide.

Each House may determine the Rules of its Proceedings, punish its Members for disorderly Behavior, and, with the Concurrence of two thirds, expel a Member.

Each House shall keep a Journal of its Proceedings, and from time to time publish the same, excepting such Parts as may in their Judgment require Secrecy; and the Yeas and Nays of the Members of either House on any question shall, at the Desire of one fifth of those Present, be entered on the Journal.

Neither House, during the Session of Congress, shall, without the Consent of the other, adjourn for more than three days, nor to any other Place than that in which the two Houses shall be sitting.

SECTION 6. The Senators and Representatives shall receive a Compensation for their Services, to be ascertained by Law, and paid out of the Treasury of the United States. They shall in all Cases, except Treason, Felony and Breach of the Peace, be privileged from Arrest during their Attendance at the Session of their respective Houses, and in going to and returning from the same; and for any Speech or Debate in either House, they shall not be questioned in any other Place.

No Senator or Representative shall, during the Time for which he was elected, be appointed to any civil Office under the Authority of the United States, which shall have been created, or the Emoluments whereof shall have been increased during such time; and no Person holding any Office under the United States, shall be a Member of either House during his Continuance in Office.

SECTION 7. All Bills for raising Revenue shall originate in the House of Representatives; but the Senate may propose or concur with Amendments as on other Bills.

Every Bill which shall have passed the House of Representatives and the Senate, shall, before it become a Law, be presented to the President of the United States: If he approve he shall sign it, but if not he shall return it, with his Objections to that House in which it shall have originated, who shall enter the Objections at large on their Journal, and proceed to reconsider it. If after such Reconsideration two thirds of that House shall agree to pass the Bill, it shall be sent, together with the Objections, to the other House, by which it shall likewise be reconsidered, and if approved by two thirds of that House, it shall become a Law. But in all such Cases the Votes of both Houses shall be determined by yeas and Nays, and the Names of the Persons voting for and against the Bill shall be entered on the Journal of each House respectively. If any Bill shall not be returned by the President within ten Days (Sundays excepted) after it shall have been presented to him, the Same shall be a Law, in like Manner as if he had signed it, unless the Congress by their Adjournment prevent its Return, in which Case it shall not be a Law.

Every Order, Resolution, or Vote to which the Concurrence of the Senate and House of Representatives may be necessary (except on a question of Adjournment) shall be presented to the President of the United States; and before the Same shall take Effect, shall be approved by him, or being disapproved by him, shall be re-passed by two thirds of the Senate and House of Representatives, according to the Rules and Limitations prescribed in the Case of a Bill.

SECTION 8. The Congress shall have Power To lay and collect Taxes, Duties, Imposts and Excises, to pay the Debts and provide for the common Defense and general Welfare of the United States; but all Duties, Imposts and Excises shall be uniform throughout the United States;

❖ To borrow Money on the credit of the United States;

❖ To regulate Commerce with foreign Nations, and among the several States, and with the Indian Tribes;

❖ To establish an uniform Rule of Naturalization, and uniform Laws on the subject of Bankruptcies throughout the United States;

❖ To coin Money, regulate the Value thereof, and of foreign Coin, and fix the Standard of Weights and Measures;

❖ To provide for the Punishment of counterfeiting the Securities and current Coin of the United States;

❖ To establish Post Offices and post Roads;

❖ To promote the Progress of Science and useful Arts, by securing for limited Times to Authors and Inventors the exclusive Right to their respective Writings and Discoveries;

❖ To constitute Tribunals inferior to the su-preme Court;

❖ To define and punish Piracies and Felo-nies committed on the high Seas, and Offences against the Law of Nations;

❖ To declare War, grant Letters of Mar-quee and Reprisal, and make Rules concerning Captures on Land and Water;

❖ To raise and support Armies, but no Ap-propriation of Money to that Use shall be for a longer Term than two Years;

❖ To provide and maintain a Navy;

❖ To make Rules for the Government and Regulation of the land and naval Forces;

❖ To provide for calling forth the Militia to execute the Laws of the Union, suppress Insurrec-tions and repel Invasions;

❖ To provide for organizing, arming, and disciplining, the Militia, and for governing such Part of them as may be employed in the Service of the United States, reserving to the States respec-tively, the Appointment of the Officers, and the Authority of training the Militia according to the discipline prescribed by Congress;

❖ To exercise exclusive Legislation in all Cases whatsoever, over such District (not exceeding ten Miles square) as may, by Cession of particular States, and the Acceptance of Congress, become the Seat of the Government of the United States, and to exercise like Authority over all Places purchased by the Consent of the Legislature of the State in which the Same shall be, for the Erection of Forts, Magazines, Arsenals, dock-Yards, and other needful Buildings;--And

❖ To make all Laws which shall be necessary and proper for carrying into Execution the foregoing Powers, and all other Powers vested by this Constitution in the Government of the United States, or in any Department or Officer thereof.

SECTION 9. The Migration or Importation of such Persons as any of the States now existing shall think proper to admit, shall not be prohibited by the Congress prior to the Year one thousand eight hundred and eight, but a Tax or duty may be imposed on such Importation, not exceeding ten dollars for each Person.

The Privilege of the Writ of Habeas Corpus shall not be suspended, unless when in Cases of Rebellion or Invasion the public Safety may require it.

No Bill of Attainder or ex post facto Law shall be passed.

No Capitation, or other direct, Tax shall be laid, <u>unless in Proportion to the Census or enumeration herein before directed to be taken</u>.

No Tax or Duty shall be laid on Articles exported from any State.

No Preference shall be given by any Regulation of Commerce or Revenue to the Ports of one State over those of another; nor shall Vessels bound to, or from, one State, be obliged to enter, clear, or pay Duties in another.

No Money shall be drawn from the Treasury, but in Consequence of Appropriations made by Law; and a regular Statement and Account of the Receipts and Expenditures of all public Money shall be published from time to time.

No Title of Nobility shall be granted by the United States: And no Person holding any Office of Profit or Trust under them, shall, without the Consent of the Congress, accept of any present, Emolument, Office, or Title, of any kind whatever, from any King, Prince, or foreign State.

SECTION 10. No State shall enter into any Treaty, Alliance, or Confederation; grant Letters of Marquee and Reprisal; coin Money; emit Bills of Credit; make any Thing but gold and silver Coin a Tender in Payment of Debts; pass any Bill of Attainder, ex post facto Law, or Law impairing the Obligation of Contracts, or grant any Title of Nobility.

No State shall, without the Consent of the Congress, lay any Imposts or Duties on Imports or Exports, except what may be absolutely necessary for executing it's inspection Laws: and the net Produce of all Duties and Imposts, laid by any State on Imports or Exports, shall be for the Use of the Treasury of the United States; and all such Laws shall be subject to the Revision and Control of the Congress.

No State shall, without the Consent of Congress, lay any Duty of Tonnage, keep Troops, or Ships of War in time of Peace, enter into any Agreement or Compact with another State, or with a foreign Power, or engage in War, unless actually invaded, or in such imminent Danger as will not admit of delay.

ARTICLE II.

SECTION 1. The executive Power shall be vested in a President of the United States of America. He shall hold his Office during the Term of four Years, and, together with the Vice President, chosen for the same Term, be elected, as follows:

Each State shall appoint, in such Manner as the Legislature thereof may direct, a Number of Electors, equal to the whole Number of Senators and Representatives to which the State may be entitled in the Congress: but no Senator or Representative, or Person holding an Office of Trust or Profit under the United States, shall be appointed an Elector.

The Electors shall meet in their respective States, and vote by Ballot for two Persons, of whom one at least shall not be an Inhabitant of the same State with themselves. And they shall make a List of all the Persons voted for, and of the Number of Votes for each; which List they shall sign and certify, and transmit sealed to the Seat of the Government of the United States, directed to the President of the Senate. The President of the Senate shall, in the Presence of the Senate and House of Representatives, open all the Certificates, and the Votes shall then be counted. The Person having the greatest Number of Votes shall be the President, if such Number be a Majority of the whole Number of Electors appointed; and if there be more than one who have such Majority, and have an equal Number of Votes, then the House of Representatives shall immediately chuse by Ballot one of them for President; and if no Person have a Majority, then from the five highest on the List the said House shall in like Manner chuse the President. But in chusing the President, the Votes shall be taken by States, the Representation from each State having one Vote; A quorum for this purpose shall consist of a Member or Members from two thirds of the States, and a Majority of all the States shall be necessary to a Choice. In every Case, after the Choice of the President, the Person having the greatest Number of Votes of the Electors shall be the Vice President. But if there should remain two or more who have equal Votes, the Senate shall chuse from them by Ballot the Vice President.

The Congress may determine the Time of choosing the Electors, and the Day on which they shall give their Votes; which Day shall be the same throughout the United States.

No Person except a natural born Citizen, or a Citizen of the United States, at the time of the Adoption of this Constitution, shall be eligible to the Office of President; neither shall any Person be eligible to that Office who shall not have attained to the Age of thirty five Years, and been fourteen Years a Resident within the United States.

In Case of the Removal of the President from Office, or of his Death, Resignation, or Inability to discharge the Powers and Duties of the said Office, the Same shall devolve on the Vice President, and the Congress may by Law provide for the Case of Removal, Death, Resignation or Inability, both of the President and Vice President, declaring what Officer shall then act as President, and such Officer shall act accordingly, until the Disability be removed, or a President shall be elected.

The President shall, at stated Times, receive for his Services, a Compensation, which shall neither be increased nor diminished during the Period for which he shall have been elected, and he shall not receive within that Period any other Emolument from the United States, or any of them.

Before he enter on the Execution of his Office, he shall take the following Oath or Affirmation:--"I do solemnly swear (or affirm) that I will faithfully execute the Office of President of the United States, and will to the best of my Ability, preserve, protect and defend the Constitution of the United States."

SECTION 2. The President shall be Commander in Chief of the Army and Navy of the United States, and of the Militia of the several States, when called into the actual Service of the United States; he may require the Opinion, in writing, of the principal Officer in each of the executive Departments, upon any Subject relating to the Duties of their respective Offices, and he shall have Power to grant Reprieves and Pardons for Offences against the United States, except in Cases of Impeachment.

He shall have Power, by and with the Advice and Consent of the Senate, to make Treaties, provided two thirds of the Senators present concur; and he shall nominate, and by and with the Advice and Consent of the Senate, shall appoint Ambassadors, other public Ministers and Consuls, Judges of the supreme Court, and all other Officers of the United States, whose Appointments are not herein otherwise provided for, and which shall be established by Law: but the Congress may by Law vest the Appointment of such inferior Officers, as they think proper, in the President alone, in the Courts of Law, or in the Heads of Departments.

The President shall have Power to fill up all Vacancies that may happen during the Recess of the Senate, by granting Commissions which shall expire at the End of their next Session.

SECTION 3. He shall from time to time give to the Congress Information of the State of the Union, and recommend to their Consideration such Measures as he shall judge necessary and expedient; he may, on extraordinary Occasions, convene both Houses, or either of them, and in Case of Disagreement between them, with Respect to the Time of Adjournment, he may adjourn them to such Time as he shall think proper; he shall receive Ambassadors and other public Ministers; he shall take Care that the Laws be faithfully executed, and shall Commission all the Officers of the United States.

SECTION.4. The President, Vice President and all civil Officers of the United States, shall be removed from Office on Impeachment for, and Conviction of, Treason, Bribery, or other high Crimes and Misdemeanors.

ARTICLE III.

SECTION 1. The judicial Power of the United States shall be vested in one supreme Court, and in such inferior Courts as the Congress may from time to time ordain and establish. The Judges, both of the supreme and inferior Courts, shall hold their Offices during good Behavior, and shall, at stated Times, receive for their Services a Compensation, which shall not be diminished during their Continuance in Office.

SECTION 2. The judicial Power shall extend to all Cases, in Law and Equity, arising under this Constitution, the Laws of the United States, and Treaties made, or which shall be made, under their Authority;--to all Cases affecting Ambassadors, other public Ministers and Consuls;--to all Cases of admiralty and maritime Jurisdiction;--to Controversies to which the United States shall be a Party;--to Controversies between two or more States;-- between a State and Citizens of another State;--between Citizens of different States;--between Citizens of the same State claiming Lands under Grants of different States, and between a State, or the Citizens thereof, and foreign States, Citizens or Subjects.

In all Cases affecting Ambassadors, other public Ministers and Consuls, and those in which a State shall be Party, the supreme Court shall have original Jurisdiction. In all the other Cases before mentioned, the supreme Court shall have appellate Jurisdiction, both as to Law and Fact, with such Exceptions, and under such Regulations as the Congress shall make.

The Trial of all Crimes, except in Cases of Impeachment, shall be by Jury; and such Trial shall be held in the State where the said Crimes shall have been committed; but when not committed within any State, the Trial shall be at such Place or Places as the Congress may by Law have directed.

SECTION 3. Treason against the United States, shall consist only in levying War against them, or in adhering to their Enemies, giving them Aid and Comfort. No Person shall be convicted of Treason unless on the Testimony of two Witnesses to the same overt Act, or on Confession in open Court.

The Congress shall have Power to declare the Punishment of Treason, but no Attainder of Treason shall work Corruption of Blood, or Forfeiture except during the Life of the Person attainted.

ARTICLE. IV.

SECTION 1. Full Faith and Credit shall be given in each State to the public Acts, Records, and judicial

Proceedings of every other State. And the Congress may by general Laws prescribe the Manner in which such Acts, Records and Proceedings shall be proved, and the Effect thereof.

SECTION 2. The Citizens of each State shall be entitled to all Privileges and Immunities of Citizens in the several States.

A Person charged in any State with Treason, Felony, or other Crime, who shall flee from Justice, and be found in another State, shall on Demand of the executive Authority of the State from which he fled, be delivered up, to be removed to the State having Jurisdiction of the Crime.

No Person held to Service or Labor in one State, under the Laws thereof, escaping into another, shall, in Consequence of any Law or Regulation therein, be discharged from such Service or Labour, but shall be delivered up on Claim of the Party to whom such Service or Labour may be due.

SECTION 3. New States may be admitted by the Congress into this Union; but no new State shall be formed or erected within the Jurisdiction of any other State; nor any State be formed by the Junction of two or more States, or Parts of States, without the Consent of the Legislatures of the States concerned as well as of the Congress. The Congress shall have Power to dispose of and make all needful Rules and

Regulations respecting the Territory or other Property belonging to the United States; and nothing in this Constitution shall be so construed as to Prejudice any Claims of the United States, or of any particular State.

SECTION 4. The United States shall guarantee to every State in this Union a Republican Form of Government, and shall protect each of them against Invasion; and on Application of the Legislature, or of the Executive (when the Legislature cannot be convened), against domestic Violence.

ARTICLE V.

The Congress, whenever two thirds of both Houses shall deem it necessary, shall propose Amendments to this Constitution, or, on the Application of the Legislatures of two thirds of the several States, shall call a Convention for proposing Amendments, which, in either Case, shall be valid to all Intents and Purposes, as Part of this Constitution, when ratified by the Legislatures of three fourths of the several States, or by Conventions in three fourths thereof, as the one or the other Mode of Ratification may be proposed by the Congress; Provided that no Amendment which may be made prior to the Year One thousand eight hundred and eight shall in any Manner affect the first and fourth Clauses in the Ninth Section of the first Article; and that no State, without its Consent, shall be deprived of its equal Suffrage in the Senate.

ARTICLE VI.

All Debts contracted and Engagements entered into, before the Adoption of this Constitution, shall be as valid against the United States under this Constitution, as under the Confederation.

This Constitution, and the Laws of the United States which shall be made in Pursuance thereof; and all Treaties made, or which shall be made, under the Authority of the United States, shall be the supreme Law of the Land; and the Judges in every State shall be bound thereby, any Thing in the Constitution or Laws of any State to the Contrary notwithstanding.

The Senators and Representatives before mentioned, and the Members of the several State Legislatures, and all executive and judicial Officers, both of the United States and of the several States, shall be bound by Oath or Affirmation, to support this Constitution; but no religious Test shall ever be required as a Qualification to any Office or public Trust under the United States.

ARTICLE VII.

The Ratification of the Conventions of nine States shall be sufficient for the Establishment of this Constitution between the States so ratifying the Same.

The Word, "the," being interlined between the seventh and eighth Lines of the first Page, the Word "Thirty" being partly written on an Erasure in the fifteenth Line of the first Page, The Words "is tried" being interlined between the thirty second and thirty third Lines of the first Page and the Word "the" being interlined between the forty third and forty fourth Lines of the second Page.

Attest: *William Jackson* *Secretary*

Done in Convention by the Unanimous Consent of the States present the Seventeenth Day of September in the Year of our Lord one thousand seven hundred and Eighty seven and of the Independence of the United States of America the Twelfth In witness whereof We have hereunto subscribed our Names,

G. Washington
President and deputy from Virginia

States of America the Twelfth In witness whereof We have hereunto subscribed our Names,

DELAWARE

Geo: Read
Gunning Bedford jun
John Dickinson
Richard Bassett
Jaco: Broom

MARYLAND

James McHenry
Dan of St Thos. Jenifer
Danl. Carroll

VIRGINIA

John Blair
James Madison Jr.

NORTH CAROLINA

Wm. Blount
Richd. Dobbs Spaight
Hu Williamson

SOUTH CAROLINA

J. Rutledge
Charles Cotesworth Pinckney
Charles Pinckney
Pierce Butler

GEORGIA

William Few
Abr Baldwin

NEW HAMPSHIRE

John Langdon
Nicholas Gilman

MASSACHUSETTS

Nathaniel Gorham
Rufus King

CONNECTICUT

Wm. Saml. Johnson
Roger Sherman

NEW YORK

Alexander Hamilton

NEW JERSEY

Wil: Livingston
David Brearley
Wm. Paterson
Jona: Dayton

PENNSYLVANIA

B Franklin
Thomas Mifflin
Robt. Morris
Geo. Clymer
Thos. FitzSimons
Jared Ingersoll
James Wilson
Gouv Morris

AMENDMENTS I - X
THE BILL OF RIGHTS

A Transcription

Note: The following text is a transcription of the first ten amendments to the Constitution of the United States in their original form. These amendments were ratified December 15, 1791, and form what is known as the "Bill of Rights."

AMENDMENT I

Congress shall make no law respecting an establishment of religion, or prohibiting the free exercise thereof; or abridging the freedom of speech, or of the press; or the right of the people peaceably to assemble, and to petition the Government for a redress of grievances.

AMENDMENT II

A well regulated Militia, being necessary to the security of a free State, the right of the people to keep and bear Arms, shall not be infringed.

AMENDMENT III

No Soldier shall, in time of peace be quartered in any house, without the consent of the Owner, nor in time of war, but in a manner to be prescribed by law.

AMENDMENT IV

The right of the people to be secure in their persons, houses, papers, and effects, against unreasonable searches and seizures, shall not be violated, and no Warrants shall issue, but upon probable cause, supported by Oath or affirmation, and particularly describing the place to be searched, and the persons or things to be seized.

AMENDMENT V

No person shall be held to answer for a capital, or otherwise infamous crime, unless on a presentment or indictment of a Grand Jury, except in cases arising in the land or naval forces, or in the Militia, when in actual service in time of War or public danger; nor shall any person be subject for the same offence to be twice put in jeopardy of life or limb; nor shall be compelled in any criminal case to be a witness against himself, nor be deprived of life, liberty, or property, without due process of law; nor shall private property be taken for public use, without just compensation.

AMENDMENT VI

In all criminal prosecutions, the accused shall enjoy the right to a speedy and public trial, by an impartial jury of the State and district wherein the crime shall have been committed, which district shall have been previously ascertained by law, and to be informed of the nature and cause of the accusation; to be confronted with the witnesses against him; to have compulsory process for obtaining witnesses in his favor, and to have the Assistance of Counsel for his defense.

AMENDMENT VII

In Suits at common law, where the value in controversy shall exceed twenty dollars, the right of trial by jury shall be preserved, and no fact tried by a jury, shall be otherwise re-examined in any Court of the United States, than according to the rules of the common law.

AMENDMENT VIII

Excessive bail shall not be required, nor excessive fines imposed, nor cruel and unusual punishments inflicted.

AMENDMENT IX

The enumeration in the Constitution, of certain rights, shall not be construed to deny or disparage others retained by the people.

AMENDMENT X

The powers not delegated to the United States by the Constitution, nor prohibited by it to the States, are reserved to the States respectively, or to the people.

AMENDMENTS XI – XXVII TO THE CONSTITUTION OF THE UNITED STATES OF AMERICA

AMENDMENT XI

Note: Article III, section 2, of the Constitution was modified by amendment XI.

The Judicial power of the United States shall not be construed to extend to any suit in law or equity, commenced or prosecuted against one of the United States by Citizens of another State, or by Citizens or Subjects of any Foreign State.

Passed by Congress; March 4, 1794
Ratified; February 7, 1795

AMENDMENT XII

Note: A portion of Article II, section 1 of the Constitution was superseded by the 12th amendment.

The Electors shall meet in their respective states and vote by ballot for President and Vice-President, one of whom, at least, shall not be an inhabitant of the same state with themselves; they shall name in their ballots the person voted for as President, and in distinct ballots the person voted for as

Vice-President, and they shall make distinct lists of all persons voted for as President, and of all persons voted for as Vice-President, and of the number of votes for each, which lists they shall sign and certify, and transmit sealed to the seat of the government of the United States, directed to the President of the Senate; -- the President of the Senate shall, in the presence of the Senate and House of Representatives, open all the certificates and the votes shall then be counted; -- The person having the greatest number of votes for President, shall be the President, if such number be a majority of the whole number of Electors appointed; and if no person have such majority, then from the persons having the highest numbers not exceeding three on the list of those voted for as President, the House of Representatives shall choose immediately, by ballot, the President. But in choosing the President, the votes shall be taken by states, the representation from each state having one vote; a quorum for this purpose shall consist of a member or members from two-thirds of the states and a majority of all the states shall be necessary to a choice.

[And if the House of Representatives shall not choose a President whenever the right of choice shall devolve upon them, before the fourth day of March next following, then the Vice-President shall act as President, as in case of the death or other constitutional disability of the President. --]* *Superseded by section 3 of the 20th amendment.*

The person having the greatest number of votes as Vice-President, shall be the Vice-President, if such number be a majority of the whole number of Electors appointed, and if no person have a majority, then from the two highest numbers on the list, the Senate shall choose the Vice-President; a quorum for the purpose shall consist of two-thirds of the whole number of Senators, and a majority of the whole number shall be necessary to a choice. But no person constitutionally ineligible to the office of President shall be eligible to that of Vice-President of the United States.

Passed by Congress; December 9, 1803
Ratified; June 15, 1804

AMENDMENT XIII

Note: A portion of Article IV, section 2, of the Constitution was superseded by the 13th amendment.

SECTION 1. Either slavery, nor involuntary servitude, except as a punishment for crime whereof the party shall have been duly convicted, shall exist within the United States, or any place subject to their jurisdiction.

SECTION 2. Congress shall have power to enforce this article by appropriate legislation.

Passed by Congress; January 31, 1865
Ratified; December 6, 1865

AMENDMENT XIV

Note: Article I, section 2, of the Constitution was modified by section 2 of the 14th amendment.

SECTION 1. All persons born or naturalized in the United States, and subject to the jurisdiction thereof, are citizens of the United States and of the State wherein they reside. No State shall make or enforce any law which shall abridge the privileges or immunities of citizens of the United States; nor shall any State deprive any person of life, liberty, or property, without due process of law; nor deny to any person within its jurisdiction the equal protection of the laws.

SECTION 2. Representatives shall be apportioned among the several States according to their respective numbers, counting the whole number of persons in each State, excluding Indians not taxed. But when the right to vote at any election for the choice of electors for President and Vice-President of the United States, Representatives in Congress, the Executive and Judicial officers of a State, or the members of the Legislature thereof, is denied to any of the male inhabitants of such State, being twenty-one

years of age, (*Changed by section 1 of the 26th amendment.*) and citizens of the United States, or in any way abridged, except for participation in rebellion, or other crime, the basis of representation therein shall be reduced in the proportion which the number of such male citizens shall bear to the whole number of male citizens twenty-one years of age in such State.

SECTION 3. No person shall be a Senator or Representative in Congress, or elector of President and Vice-President, or hold any office, civil or military, under the United States, or under any State, who, having previously taken an oath, as a member of Congress, or as an officer of the United States, or as a member of any State legislature, or as an executive or judicial officer of any State, to support the Constitution of the United States, shall have engaged in insurrection or rebellion against the same, or given aid or comfort to the enemies thereof. But Congress may by a vote of two-thirds of each House, remove such disability.

SECTION 4. The validity of the public debt of the United States, authorized by law, including debts incurred for payment of pensions and bounties for services in suppressing insurrection or rebellion, shall not be questioned. But neither the United States nor any State shall assume or pay any debt or obligation incurred in aid of insurrection or rebellion against the United States, or any claim for the loss or emancipation of any slave; but all such debts, obligations and claims shall be held illegal and void.

SECTION 5. The Congress shall have the power to enforce, by appropriate legislation, the provisions of this article.

Passed by Congress June 13, 1866
Ratified July 9, 1868.

AMENDMENT XV

SECTION 1. The right of citizens of the United States to vote shall not be denied or abridged by the United States or by any State on account of race, color, or previous condition of servitude.

SECTION 2. The Congress shall have the power to enforce this article by appropriate legislation.

Passed by Congress February 26, 1869
Ratified February 3, 1870

AMENDMENT XVI

Note: Article I, section 9, of the Constitution was modified by amendment 16.

The Congress shall have power to lay and collect taxes on incomes, from whatever source derived, without apportionment among the several States, and without regard to any census or enumeration.

Passed by Congress July 2, 1909
Ratified February 3, 1913

AMENDMENT XVII

Note: Article I, section 3, of the Constitution was modified by the 17th amendment.

The Senate of the United States shall be composed of two Senators from each State, elected by the people thereof, for six years; and each Senator shall have one vote. The electors in each State shall have the qualifications requisite for electors of the most numerous branch of the State legislatures.

When vacancies happen in the representation of any State in the Senate, the executive authority of such State shall issue writs of election to fill such vacancies: provided, that the legislature of any State may empower the executive thereof to make temporary appointments until the people fill the vacancies by election as the legislature may direct.

This amendment shall not be so construed as to affect the election or term of any Senator chosen before it becomes valid as part of the Constitution.

Passed by Congress May 13, 1912
Ratified April 8, 1913.

AMENDMENT XVIII

SECTION 1. After one year from the ratification of this article the manufacture, sale, or transportation of intoxicating liquors within, the importation thereof into, or the exportation thereof from the United States and all territory subject to the jurisdiction thereof for beverage purposes is hereby prohibited.

SECTION 2. The Congress and the several States shall have concurrent power to enforce this article by appropriate legislation.

SECTION 3. This article shall be inoperative unless it shall have been ratified as an amendment to the Constitution by the legislatures of the several States, as provided in the Constitution, within seven years from the date of the submission hereof to the States by the Congress.

Passed by Congress December 18, 1917
Ratified January 16, 1919
Repealed by amendment 21

AMENDMENT XIX

The right of citizens of the United States to vote shall not be denied or abridged by the United States or by any State on account of sex.

Congress shall have power to enforce this article by appropriate legislation.

Passed by Congress June 4, 1919
Ratified August 18, 1920.

AMENDMENT XX

Note: Article I, section 4, of the Constitution was modified by section 2 of this amendment. In addition, a portion of the 12th amendment was superseded by section 3.

SECTION 1. The terms of the President and the Vice President shall end at noon on the 20th day of January, and the terms of Senators and Representatives at noon on the 3rd day of January, of the years in which such

terms would have ended if this article had not been ratified; and the terms of their successors shall then begin.

SECTION 2. The Congress shall assemble at least once in every year, and such meeting shall begin at noon on the 3d day of January, unless they shall by law appoint a different day.

SECTION 3. If, at the time fixed for the beginning of the term of the President, the President elect shall have died, the Vice President elect shall become President. If a President shall not have been chosen before the time fixed for the beginning of his term, or if the President elect shall have failed to qualify, then the Vice President elect shall act as President until a President shall have qualified; and the Congress may by law provide for the case wherein neither a President elect nor a Vice President shall have qualified, declaring who shall then act as President, or the manner in which one who is to act shall be selected, and such person shall act accordingly until a President or Vice President shall have qualified.

SECTION 4. The Congress may by law provide for the case of the death of any of the persons from whom the House of Representatives may choose a President whenever the right of choice shall have devolved upon them, and for the case of the death of any of the persons from whom the Senate may choose a Vice President whenever the right of choice shall have devolved upon them.

SECTION 5. Sections 1 and 2 shall take effect on the 15th day of October following the ratification of this article.

SECTION 6. This article shall be inoperative unless it shall have been ratified as an amendment to the Constitution by the legislatures of three-fourths of the several States within seven years from the date of its submission.

Passed by Congress March 2, 1932
Ratified January 23, 1933

AMENDMENT XXI

SECTION 1. The eighteenth article of amendment to the Constitution of the United States is hereby repealed.

SECTION 2. The transportation or importation into any State, Territory, or Possession of the

United States for delivery or use therein of intoxicating liquors, in violation of the laws thereof, is hereby prohibited.

SECTION 3. This article shall be inoperative unless it shall have been ratified as an amendment to the Constitution by conventions in the several States, as provided in the Constitution, within seven years from the date of the submission hereof to the States by the Congress.

Passed by Congress February 20, 1933
Ratified December 5, 1933

AMENDMENT XXII

SECTION 1. No person shall be elected to the office of the President more than twice, and no person who has held the office of President, or acted as President, for more than two years of a term to which some other person was elected President shall be elected to the office of President more than once. But this Article shall not apply to any person holding the office of President when this Article was proposed by Congress, and shall not prevent any person who may be holding the office of President, or acting as President, during the term within which this Article becomes operative from holding the office of President or acting as President during the remainder of such term.

SECTION 2. This article shall be inoperative unless it shall have been ratified as an amendment to the Constitution by the legislatures of three-fourths of the several States within seven years from the date of its submission to the States by the Congress.

Passed by Congress March 21, 1947
Ratified February 27, 1951

AMENDMENT XXIII

SECTION 1. The District constituting the seat of Government of the United States shall appoint in such manner as Congress may direct:

A number of electors of President and Vice President equal to the whole number of Senators and Representatives in Congress to which the District would be entitled if it were a State, but in no event more than the least populous State; they shall be in addition to those appointed by the States, but they shall be considered, for the purposes of the election of President and Vice President, to be electors appointed by a State; and they shall meet in the District and perform such duties as provided by the twelfth article of amendment.

SECTION 2. The Congress shall have power to enforce this article by appropriate legislation.

Passed by Congress; June 16, 1960
Ratified; March 29, 1961

AMENDMENT XXIV

SECTION 1.   The right of citizens of the United States to vote in any primary or other election for President or Vice President, for electors for President or Vice President, or for Senator or Representative in Congress, shall not be denied or abridged by the United States or any State by reason of failure to pay poll tax or other tax.

SECTION 2.   The Congress shall have power to enforce this article by appropriate legislation.

Passed by Congress August 27, 1962
Ratified January 23, 1964

AMENDMENT XXV

Note: Article II, section 1, of the Constitution was affected by the 25th amendment.

SECTION 1.   In case of the removal of the President from office or of his death or resignation, the Vice President shall become President.

SECTION 2.   Whenever there is a vacancy in the office of the Vice President, the President shall nominate a Vice President who shall take office upon confirmation by a majority vote of both Houses of Congress.

SECTION 3.   Whenever the President transmits to the President pro tempore of the Senate and the Speaker of the House of Representatives his written declaration that he is unable to discharge the powers and duties of his office, and until he transmits to them a written declaration to the contrary, such powers and duties shall be discharged by the Vice President as Acting President.

SECTION 4. Whenever the Vice President and a majority of either the principal officers of the executive departments or of such other body as Congress may by law provide, transmit to the President pro tempore of the Senate and the Speaker of the House of Representatives their written declaration that the President is unable to discharge the powers and duties of his office, the Vice President shall immediately assume the powers and duties of the office as Acting President.

Thereafter, when the President transmits to the President pro tempore of the Senate and the Speaker of the House of Representatives his written declaration that no inability exists, he shall resume the powers and duties of his office unless the Vice President and a majority of either the principal officers of the executive department or of such other body as Congress may by law provide, transmit within four days to the President pro tempore of the Senate and the Speaker of the House of Representatives their written declaration that the President is unable to discharge the powers and duties of his office. Thereupon Congress shall decide the issue, assembling within forty-eight hours for that purpose if not in session. If the

Congress, within twenty-one days after receipt of the latter written declaration, or, if Congress is not in session, within twenty-one days after Congress is required to assemble, determines by two-thirds vote of both Houses that the President is unable to discharge the powers and duties of his office, the Vice President shall continue to discharge the same as Acting President; otherwise, the President shall resume the powers and duties of his office.

Passed by Congress July 6, 1965
Ratified February 10, 1967

AMENDMENT XXVI

Note: Amendment 14, section 2, of the Constitution was modified by section 1 of the 26th amendment.

SECTION 1. The right of citizens of the United States, who are eighteen years of age or older, to vote shall not be denied or abridged by the United States or by any State on account of age.

SECTION 2. The Congress shall have power to enforce this article by appropriate legislation.

Passed by Congress March 23, 1971
and Ratified July 1, 1971

AMENDMENT XXVII

No law, varying the compensation for the services of the Senators and Representatives, shall take effect, until an election of representatives shall have intervened.

Originally Proposed at September 25, 1989
and Ratified May 7, 1992

www.ingramcontent.com/pod-product-compliance
Lightning Source LLC
Chambersburg PA
CBHW022249290526

45785CB00015B/409